ORACLE QUICK GUIDES
PART 2 - ORACLE DATABASE DESIGN

Malcolm Coxall

Edited by Guy Caswell

Cornelio
Books

Published by M.Coxall - Cornelio Books
Copyright 2013 -2014 Malcolm Coxall
First Published in Spain, United Kingdom 2013
ISBN: 978-84-941783-6-8

"Space does not exist unless there are objects in it

Nor does time exist without events."

Contents

Preface and Audience

About the Author

Preface and Audience

Oracle Quick Guides: Welcome to Oracle Quick Guides, a series of quick learning guides for Oracle designers, developers and managers.

Guide Audience: These guides are designed to rapidly deliver key information about Oracle to the following audience groups:

- Project Managers, Team Leaders and Testers who are new to Oracle and need rapid access to strategic information about the Oracle development environment.
- Business Analysts, Designers and Software Developers who are new to Oracle and need to make a first step in gaining a detailed understanding of the design and development issues involved in Oracle.

Guide Contents: These guides have been divided by subject matter. They become increasingly complex and more specific the later the volume. Thus, part 1 is quite general but later volumes are very technical and specific. Here, part 2 introduces new entrants to concepts of Oracle database analysis and design, database normalisation, the logical data model, E-R modelling and diagrams, logical to physical transformation in Oracle Designer, physical database design, de-normalization, database design for performance, and building a physical database from a server model.

Our Objective: There are plenty of Oracle textbooks on the market. Most of them are huge and only partly relevant to a particular group of readers. Therefore, we decided to divide the subject into smaller, more targeted volumes in order that you only get the information YOU need. For example, a Project Manager doesn't need to know some of the more esoteric programming tips, but will need to know some of the strategic issues affecting design and testing. In a similar way, a Programmer is much more interested in the syntactic details than in the strategic issues affecting the choice of an Oracle upgrade path.

And so we target these guides at particular groups with specific interests and we try to avoid overloading the reader with too much detail or extraneous material.

Assumptions: We assume that the reader will be using Oracle 9i, 10g or 11g, Oracle Designer 10g, and employing a standard RAD development methodology.

---oOo---

1. The Analysis phase - Separating Functional and Database Design

The first step in Oracle RDBMS system analysis and design is establishing the separation between Database design and Functional (software) design. This needs to be done with some care because, in an Oracle database, many elements of data validation and execution occur at the database level rather than in a piece of external software code. This is a fundamental difference between traditional 3G software developments and the design and development in an Object Relational environment, like Oracle.

Oracle is a so-called Object Relational database and this means that much default validation behaviour is actually embedded in the database itself. A design team leader needs to constantly decide the appropriate place for software code to reside and execute, i.e. in the database as a "trigger" or as a piece of external code executed on demand against the database.

Generally, the rule is that as much code as possible is associated with the tables within the database when the code is considered to have a low volatility (i.e. the software functionality hardly ever changes). Software which is more volatile and prone to change is generally excluded from being embedded at the database level.

Logically, software embedded in the database tends to represent those immutable properties which define the business rules inherent in the database object itself. For example, it would be illogical if an order number was *not unique* in a database: order numbers are unique; otherwise an order cannot be identified.

Therefore, the concept of guaranteeing unique order numbers in the ORDERS table is a good "candidate" to become part of the ORDERS inherent validation, rather than being guaranteed by some piece of external software every time an order is added, because this validation is an inherent and unchangeable part of an order.

This separation of validation and other processing between database object and external software complicates the designer's life somewhat and as a consequence, the design team lead must separate the tasks of Design and Development between the roles of database design and functional design. This also means dividing up the project into a Database Design Team and an Application (functional) development team. And it also means that the two teams need to liaise closely on where particular software functionality will reside.

This normally means that the Database Design Team need to start their Analysis and Logical design work well ahead of the Application (functional) development team, because the Application (functional) designers need to have a stable database design in place before even considering software design definitions and certainly long before any code is produced.

Here is a simplified organisation chart which indicates how roles are split between Oracle database designers and Oracle software developers:

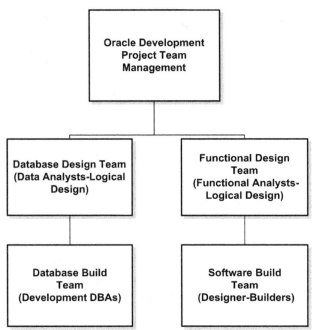

Since the purpose of this guide is to examine Database Design, we will leave functional issues for now. This is the subject of another Oracle Quick Guide, where we will consider the issues involved in logical and physical software design from Functional analysis to physical software module design and definition. For now, we will focus on the logical and physical design of an underlying Oracle database from Analysis, through Logical data modelling to Physical Database rollout.

---oOo---

2. Introduction to Data modelling and Database Design

Logical and Physical concepts of design:

2.1 Introduction: There are two clear steps involved in moving from a Business analysis stage to a physical database. Step 1 is Logical Design and Step 2 is Physical Design. Step 1 may be by-passed in some cases.

Step 1 is optional in those cases where the logical relationships are so self-evident and well-known to the designers. In such a case, a design team may choose to skip logical database design and move directly to the physical database design. This is not an uncommon strategy and can save a lot of time. However, if the application is in "new territory" for the users and the developers, and where little is known about the data and its relationships, it is important to go through the process of formal logical design together with the business users. In database design, late-breaking design changes and surprises can carry very high costs. So it generally pays off to err on the side of more logical design time with the users, rather than less.

Step 1: Logical Design:

- A Logical database design is the output from a data analysis process, together with selected users.

- The process of data analysis is generally carried out based on an initial "User Requirements Definition". During this process, a business analyst establishes the core business entities and relationships based on interviews with key business users.

- A fully-fledged technically accurate logical data model is defined after an exhaustive evaluation and verification of the business structures (and dataflows) together with the users. This involves defining details of relationships and attributes of business data.

- The final steps in the logical design stage involve the rationalisation of the data model. This includes the full normalization of the data model and the elimination of any other anomalies and redundancies.

Step 2 - Physical database design:

- A Physical database design is the output from the formal translation of the logical data definitions in Step 1, into the physical definitions of the required database objects used to implement the original "Requirements Definition".

- The Physical design process takes place based on the formal logical data model definitions concluded in Step 1.

- Physical database design converts logical design into definitions of physical database objects like tables, columns, indexes, keys and constraints: The process seeks to remove anomalies, such as repeating data and continues the process of "normalization" to achieve this.

- Physical database design considers issues of data normalization, key definitions, constraint definitions, data de-normalization, database performance issues, user and data security, physical storage issues, indexes, sequences and the implementation of embedded database triggers for cascading transactions and modelling business rules, auditing etc.

Step 3 - Building a physical database:

- After the design steps, the design definitions are used to build a physical database.

2.1.1 Outputs from Logical and Physical Design: As the analysis and design process moves along, logical objects are "translated" into physical database objects:

- Logical Design objects: There are three basic elements used in Logical Database Design: *Entity, Attribute and Relationship.*

- Physical Design objects: There are many elements involved in a physical database, but the most important, which translate from the above logical objects, are *Tables, Columns and Relational Constraints.*

We will now take a look at these Logical and Physical objects in detail.

2.2 Logical Design - The building blocks: entities, relationships, and attributes: There are three elements used in the Logical Database Design step we call Entity Relationship modelling:

2.2.1 Entity: An entity is something which is recognized as being capable of an independent existence and which can be uniquely identified. For example, an invoice header is an entity which can be uniquely identified by an Invoice Number. In a physical database, a

10

logical *entity* is equivalent to a physical *table*, in which a particular dataset is stored.

2.2.2 Attributes: An attribute is a component of an entity. For example, an Invoice Header has the following attributes: Invoice No., Invoice Date, Customer Id, etc. In a physical database, a logical *attribute* is equivalent to a physical *column* in a table. In a logical design, an attribute can be of three types:

- Unique Identifier: A UID is an attribute whose value uniquely identifies an entity instance. A UID is implemented as a Primary Key.

- Mandatory Attribute: A mandatory attribute is one whose value cannot be null.

- Optional Attribute: An optional attribute is one whose value can be null.

2.2.3 Relationships: Data in one entity may be related to data in another entity. A relationship is expressed as a verb. So for example, an invoice "consists of "several invoice lines. Invoice and invoice line are the entities and "consists of" is the relationship. A relationship in a physical database is manifested as a Foreign Key Constraint, which provides a link between a "parent" record and one or more "child" records.

2.2.3.1 Optionality of a Relationship: There are two possibilities. A relationship may be mandatory or it may be optional.

- **Mandatory Relationship:** A mandatory relationship specifies that each instance from an entity *must* be related to another instance.

- **Optional Relationship:** An optional relationship specifies that each instance from an entity *may* be related to another instance.

2.2.3.2 Cardinality (degree of a relationship): Several relationships are possible. In data modelling, the cardinality of one data table with respect to another entity is a critical aspect of database design. Relationships between entities define cardinality when explaining how each table relates to another. In the relational model, entities can be related as one of the following:

- One-to-one.

- One-to-many (or many-to-one).

- Many-to-many.

This is said to be the cardinality of a given entity in relation to another. The relationship between an Invoice Header and Invoice Lines is said to be a one-to-many relationship.

2.3 Physical Design: Translating Logical concepts to Physical objects: There are many object-types used in physical database design. Here we will examine the main logical elements and see how they are translated to physical database design objects during the Analysis and Design process:

Logical Term	Physical Database Object	Meaning
Entity	Table	A fixed database structure where data is stored, like an Invoice Headers or Employees table.
Attribute	Column	A single element of a table. For example, an invoice number column, where invoice numbers are stored within a table.
Occurrence	Record	One single data record, unique in a database.
Unique Identifier	Unique Key / Primary Key	A column (or group of columns) which uniquely identifies just one record in a table, for example, an invoice number may identify just one invoice.

Cont…

Logical Term	Physical Database Object	Meaning
Relationship	Foreign Key Constraint	A column (or group of columns) which are part of a record but which relate it to a foreign table. For example, in an Invoice Header table, a Customer id is used to relate the invoice to one single Customer in the Customers table.
E-R model and E-R diagram	Schema design and schema diagram	A Schema design and diagram represents the *physical* database design which results from the normalisation of a logical entity relationship model.

2.3.1 Physical naming rules: In a Physical database design, the following naming conventions are usually applied:

- **Table names are pluralized.** An Entity called EMPLOYEE becomes a table labelled EMPLOYEES.

- **Labelling a surrogate Primary key:** An artificial (surrogate) key defined for a table is often named to indicate that it is the primary or unique id. For example, an invoice header may have a primary key labelled INVOICE_ID. This column may be derived as the next unused value in a sequence and is therefore an artificial (surrogate) key. The rule often used here is that the surrogate key column is named as the *TABLENAME_ID*.

- **Labelling a Foreign Key to a surrogate Primary key:** A child table related to a parent table which has an artificial (surrogate) key, will be related via a foreign key equal to this artificial primary key of the parent table. For the sake of easy identification, the foreign key column in the child table is named to match the parent surrogate but substitutes "ID" for

13

"REF" (refers to). So using the example above, the foreign key column in the INVOICE_LINES table would be named INVOICE_REF. The rule used here is that the foreign key column in the child table is named as the *PARENT_TABLENAME_REF.*

- **Sequence Name:** Sequences are often used in Oracle to create artificial (surrogate) keys. Sequences generally are only used by one table and primary key and are named with a format something like this: *TABLE_ID_SEQ*

---oOo---

3. Practical Logical Design - Data-modelling

3.1 Data modelling

Definition of a data model: In the world of relational databases, the term *data model* is used to describe the data "objects" represented in an RDBMS, together with their properties and relationships.

These objects are typically "real world" concepts, such as products, suppliers, customers, and orders. A data model will consist of technical definitions of data objects like entities, attributes and relationships. It will also contain graphical representations of these objects and their relationships as a means of describing and visualising a logical data model, so that it is more easily understood by users, analysts, designers and software programmers.

A logical data model is constructed during the analysis stage of a software system development. It may be that different analysts, with different design objectives may produce a different, yet valid data model, depending on their perspective of the data. For example, a credit controller may see invoices in a different way to a shipping department.

Data models are often used as an aid to communication between the business people defining the requirements for a computer system and the technical people defining the design in response to those requirements. Entity-Relationship (E-R) diagrams are used to visualise the data used by real business processes, using a simple standardised format to visualise a data model.

According to Hoberman (2009): "A data model is a way-finding tool for both business and IT professionals, which uses a set of symbols and text to precisely explain a subset of real information to improve communication within the organization and thereby lead to a more flexible and stable application environment."

A data model explicitly determines the structure of data. Data models are specified in a data-modelling notation, which is graphical in form as an Entity-Relationship (E-R) Diagram. Data structures are also fully defined in terms of the technical definitions of the data model in the textural Entity-Relationship Model. For example, in a Logical data model, a textural description will exist which states something like "attribute A is NUMERIC, with maximum length=10 including 2 decimal places."

Let us now examine the techniques of logical data modelling in more detail.

3.2 Entity-Relationship Diagrams (ERDs)

3.2.1 Definition: An Entity-Relationship Diagram (ERD) is a representation of the logical data structures, using the relational model. There are different notation conventions used in ERDs. Oracle Designer and Oracle Data Modeller both use Barker's notation, which we will also use throughout and which is explained below. Barker's notation is known for its simplicity of use and understanding.

3.2.2 General Rules for ERDs: There are some basic analysis rules used in developing a Data model and constructing an Entity-Relationship Diagram. Bear these concepts in mind as we progress:

- Information should only appear once.

- Model no information that is derivable from other information already modelled.

- Information is in a predictable, logical place in the ERD.

3.2.3 ERD Concepts: ERDs make use of the three basic concepts of data modelling we have already described: Entity, Attribute and Relationship. Here we will describe how these are shown in Barker's notation:

3.2.3.1 Entity: An entity in an Oracle Designer ERD is displayed as a rectangular shape with the entity name (singular) in uppercase, inside the rectangle. For example, an entity referring to customers would be represented as follows:

CUSTOMER

3.2.3.2 Attribute: When attributes have been established for each entity, they are represented as follows on an ERD. Note that in Oracle Designer, an attribute which is a Unique Identifier is marked with a "#" symbol, a mandatory attribute is marked with an asterisk "*" and that an optional attribute is marked with an "O".

3.2.3.3 Relationships:
As analysis proceeds, relationships between Entities are discovered by the Business Analysts. These are then represented on an ERD as follows:

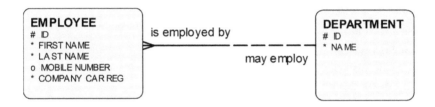

Note that the relationship will be implemented in a physical database as a Foreign Key and that the FK attribute (DEPARTMENT.ID) is not listed as an attribute in the target entity (EMPLOYEE) when building the Entity-Relationship Diagram.

3.2.3.3.1 Defining and drawing Relationships: When drawing a Relationship using the Barker's notation the following rules need to be respected:

- A relationship can exist between a maximum of two entities.

- A relationship can exist on the same entity.

- A relationship has two perspectives (a "relationship from" and a "relationship to").

- Both perspectives of a relationship must be labelled.

When defining a relationship, the following steps are used:

- Determine the entities affected by the relationship.

- Determine the optionality of the relationship.

- Determine the degree of the relationship (cardinality).

- Label the perspectives of the relationship.

3.2.3.3.2 Optionality of a Relationship:

Mandatory Relationship: A mandatory relationship specifies that each instance from an entity *must* be related to another instance. This is represented by a *straight line.*

to
_____
from

Optional Relationship: An optional relationship specifies that each instance from an entity *may* be related to another instance. This is represented by a *dashed line.*

to
— — — — — — — — — —
from

Mandatory and Optional: Relationships can be optional at one side and mandatory at the other. This is represented by a partly straight and partly dashed line:

3.2.3.3.3 Relationship Perspectives: A relationship perspective is the label at each end of the relationship line in an E-R diagram and the E-R definition itself. These perspectives always contain a verb like "employ" or "used by", "belongs to", etc. They are usually written in lower case and the label is always closest to the entity which expresses the perspective. So, a "Department may employ……. n Employee(s)" or an "Employee must be employed by ……. only one department"

Optionality: A relationship is always made up of two perspectives using the following notation:

- "Must" signifies a mandatory relationship
- "May" signifies an optional relationship

These optionalities may be used in the perspective labels or they can be omitted, since the relationship line *always* defines whether the relationship is optional or not (a solid line means the relationship is mandatory and a broken line indicates it is optional).

Cardinality (degree of a relationship): Likewise the relationship perspectives may state the cardinality of a relationship, but this is also optional in these labels: again because the E-R diagram relationship line *always* defines the cardinality:

- An employee must be employed *by one and only one department.*

- A department may employ *one or more employees.*

Advice: The main objective is to make perspective labels readable and meaningful to a business user as well as to the database designers. Therefore, it is best to exercise a bit of discretion when defining perspective labels, otherwise the E-R diagram starts to become over-complicated and read like a complex legal document, rather than being a precise but easy-to-understand representation of the business. So keep these labels short and simple.

3.2.4 Logical Naming rules: Entities are normally referred to in the singular (e.g. INVOICE). Keep the names of entities and attributes simple and easy to understand. Complicated or abbreviated entity, attribute and relationship names confuse the reader. The objective is to make a Data model easy to understand for business users and analysts, so keep the naming simple. Remember also that if you are using Oracle Designer to create your physical data model, the Designer tool will also use the entity names you provide to create foreign, primary and unique key names. So, keeping these names simple will help readability within the final build database as well. Oracle Designer will also automatically use the pluralized version of an entity name to generate the physical table name (table names are always pluralized, e.g. INVOICES).

3.3 Types of relationship

3.3.1 Introduction: In the relational model, entities (tables) can be related in any of the following ways: many-to-many, many-to-one (aka. one-to-many), or one-to-one. This is said to be the cardinality of a given table in relation to another.

We will now take a look at all of the possible relationships which can exist within a logical data model. We will review them in order of their complexity.

The reader should note that a recursive relationship is really just a variant of a "one-to-many" relationship, but it is a little bit more complicated, so we have dealt with it separately here as if it were a different type of relationship.

3.3.2 The one-to-one relationship (1:1): This is where one occurrence of an entity relates to only one occurrence in another entity.

For example, an employee is allocated a company car which can only be driven by that employee. Therefore, there is a one-to-one relationship between employee and company car. A one-to-one relationship is represented as follows in an E-R diagram:

We should note that one-to-one relationships are considered to be "unresolved" from a data rationalisation perspective. This is because 2 entities in a one-to-one relationship should really be represented as one single entity to satisfy the rules of normalization.

3.3.3 The one-to-many relationship (1:n and n:1): This is a relationship we have already encountered with our Invoice example. An invoice contains many invoice lines for the ordered products:

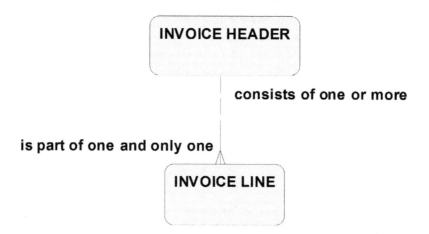

In nature and in business, there are many such "one-to-many" relationships. Orders have many order lines, bank accounts have many transactions, food products have many ingredients, hotels have many rooms etc. etc.

The one-to-many relationship is the basis of most business relational models and by far the most important relationship you will encounter in general data modelling. In normalising a logical data model with a one-to-many relationship, it is important to separate attributes according to the rules of 2nd and 3rd normal form by placing them in the correct table. So for example, an invoice line quantity would be associated with the Invoice line table and NOT the Invoice header table.

3.3.4 The many-to-many relationship (n:n): This is not an uncommon type of relationship. For example, let us consider a food company that makes a number of different finished products from a range of raw materials. Each finished product consists of a different combination of raw materials. But also, each raw material is used in several different finished products.

From a logical design point of view we can state:

- A Finished Product must contain one or many Raw Materials

AND

- A Raw Material may be used in many Finished Products

A many-to-many relationship is represented as follows in an E-R diagram:

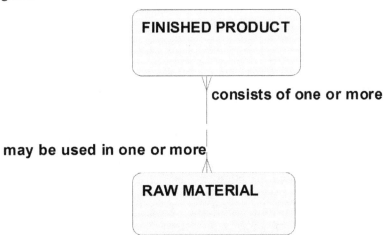

We should note that a many-to-many relationship needs to be "resolved" before it can be defined in a physical database. This resolution is carried out by defining a third entity (aka an intersect table) that contains all the combinations of UIDs from each of the 2 original entities.

3.3.5 The recursive relationship (also called a "pig's ear" - 1:n recursive): Sometimes data within an entity (table) is related to other data in the *same* table. This is not a very common relationship, but it is one that needs to be understood because it may be easily missed during analysis.

Taking a simple example, we could have a table of employees which contains all grades of employees including managers. These employees are identified using an EMPLOYEE_ID. Also, within this table we may include an attribute which indicates the EMPLOYEE_ID of each employee's manager. Every employee has a manager, so based on this we have a so-called recursive relationship, where one or more employees is related to another employee who is their manager. Or from the employee-manager's perspective, each employee may be the manager of one or more other employees. This is represented as follows in an E-R or Schema diagram:

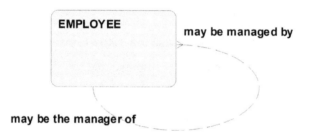

Recursive relationships are a little more complicated than relationships between two different tables (entities), but fundamentally they are the same as any other "one-to-many" relationship.

3.4 Normalization - What is it and why it is important?

3.4.1 Introduction to Normalization: One of the underlying mathematic principles in relational theory is that of normalization of data. In relational database design, normalization is a process which takes place during and after the process of Entity-Relationship modelling, where a logical data model is being transformed into a physical data model before being turned into a physical database.

Despite being so fundamental to relational design, data normalization is still widely misunderstood by Users, Analysts, Designers and Developers.

The primary objectives of data normalization are the removal of redundancy and dependency. This means that when data is inserted, updated or deleted, these processes only take place once in each table. Normalization works by dividing large entities or tables into smaller (less redundant) entities (tables) and by amalgamating entities together which have a shared one-to one relationship.

There are three concepts of data normalization referred to as "first, second and third normal form". Generally speaking, the objective of a relational database designer is to define a database which conforms to "Third Normal Form". However, there are many exceptions to this objective, which we will explore in a later chapter, when discussing database performance.

3.4.2 The benefits of normalised relational database: The benefits of a normalised relational database become very obvious when it comes to moving from a logical model to the physical database design. Here are the key benefits which are normally experienced:

3.4.2.1 Data is only stored once. The advantages of this are.

- No multiple record changes needed.

- More efficient storage

- Simple to delete or modify details.

- All records in other tables having a link to that entry will show the change.

3.4.2.2 Complex queries can be carried out: A language called SQL has been developed to allow programmers to 'Insert', 'Update', 'Delete', 'Create', 'Drop' table records. These actions are further refined by a 'Where' clause. For example

SELECT * FROM Customer WHERE CUST_ID = 2

This SQL statement will extract record number 2 from the Customer table. Far more complicated queries can be written that can extract data from many *related* tables at once. A simple example of a join within a query would be something like this:

SELECT * from ORDER_HEADER OH, CUSTOMER C
WHERE OH.CUST_REF = C.CUST_ID
AND C.CUST_ID = 2...

3.4.3 The Levels of Normalization: Here are the rules for each level of data normalization:

- **First Normal Form** states that a "Table faithfully represents a relation, primarily meaning it has at least one candidate key".

So, first normal form deals really with the "shape" of a record type. Under first normal form, all occurrences of a record type must contain the same number of fields. First normal form excludes repeating fields and groups. This basically means that repeating data must be removed from a table to remove repeating groups of data. Thus, if we had an Invoice table which incorporated invoice lines and an invoice header data in the same records, we would need to separate the data into two tables in order to make it conform to first normal form.

- **Second Normal Form** states that "no non-prime attribute in the table is functionally dependent on a proper subset of any candidate key".

So, the objective here to bring data to 2nd Normal form is to remove part key dependents, the data that is *partly* dependent on a key. For example, in our invoice lines table, we would not include the attributes "Product price" or "Product description", because these attributes ought to be part of a separate "Products" table, if our database were normalised to 2nd Normal form.

- **Third Normal Form** states that every non-prime attribute is non-transitively dependent on every candidate key in the table. The attributes that do not contribute to the description of the primary key are removed from the table. In other words, no transitive dependency is allowed.

The objective here is is to remove non-key dependences, i.e. data that is not dependent on other keys. So, are any of the attributes primarily dependent on one of the other non-key attributes rather than the design key? In our Invoice Header example the attributes: Customer Name, Address and Tax Id would be normalised by moving them into a separate Customer table. Only the Customer number would appear in the Invoice Header table, and so on.

3.5 Practical Rationalisation and Normalization steps: There are several steps in the process of rationalising and normalising the logical data model. These are the most common scenarios which must be rationalised, normalised and modelled:

- Eliminate redundant relationships.
- Resolve one-to-one relationships.

24

- Resolve many-to-many relationships.

- Grouping Entity subtypes into super type entities.

- Managing exclusive arcs.

- Managing non-Transferability of relationships.

3.5.1 Eliminate redundant relationships: It could be that information represented by a relationship can be derived from other information already being represented in an ERD. Thus, a relationship may be a "redundant" relationship.

Redundant relationships need to be removed. This can be a tricky call for a designer, especially when composite keys exist which are based on the primary key of a parent entity and its parent entity (or table). In this example, a foreign key in PERSON would contain the COUNTRY_ID and TOWN_ID.

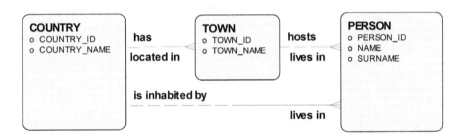

However, the relationship between COUNTRY and PERSON is redundant since the same information can be deduced from the other two relationships. This doesn't mean that other relationships between PERSON and COUNTRY cannot exist, provided they are based on different information. The model would be rationalised to appear as follows:

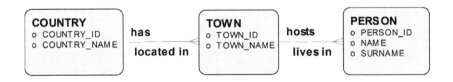

3.5.2 Resolve one-to-one relationships: A one-to-one relationship rarely exists in practice, but it can. For performance reasons it is sometimes implemented in a physical database. However, in general you must consider combining entities with a one-to-one relationship into a single entity. One-to-one relationships are resolved by amalgamating the data into a single table. In the example we showed above, the company car and employee data is rationalised from this original model:

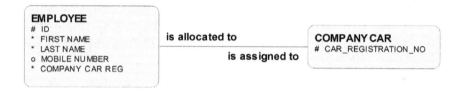

It would be rationalised into a single entity (table) EMPLOYEE which contains the mandatory attribute (column) for the COMPANY CAR registration no. Note that if the relationship had been optional, the attribute would also have been optional:

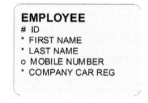

3.5.3 Resolve many-to-many relationships: A many-to-many relationship cannot exist in a physical relational database, so, during normalization, a many-to-many relationship is resolved by creating a so-called "intersect table" which contains the matching keys from both the original parent tables.

In our example of a many-to-many relationship above, the unresolved relationship is represented as follows:

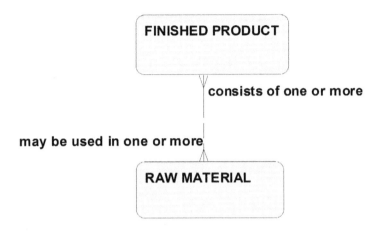

When this relationship is rationalised, a new Entity (table) called Finished-Product-Ingredient-List is created to resolve the n:n relationship. It is represented as follows:

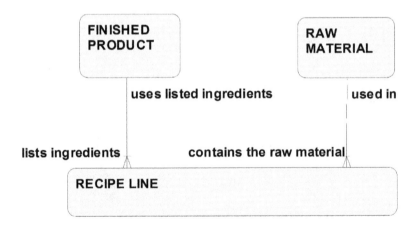

The following chart defines all possible many-to-many relationship resolutions. It is quite easy to work out from this which relationships are used where in the rationalised model.

Possible many-to-many scenarios and their resolution are summarised as follows:

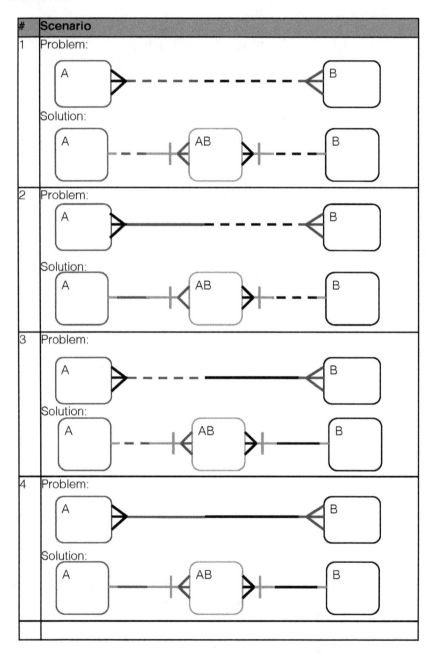

#	Scenario
1	Problem: / Solution:
2	Problem: / Solution:
3	Problem: / Solution:
4	Problem: / Solution:

3.5.4 Grouping Entity subtypes into a super type entity:

Entity Subtypes: There are many situations where different entities can be grouped together under one common entity called a super type entity, whilst the nested entities would be the subtype entities. For example, staff in a company could be categorised as:

> Administrative
> Production
> Maintenance
> Management
> Cleaning ... etc

Each of these types of staff could occupy their own separate entity.

This becomes when a super type "Staff" is created:

Rules for defining Subtypes and Supertypes: There are rules for making this kind of rationalisation, though these are quite obvious in practice:

- **Exhaustive Rule:** This rule states that every entity instance of the super type must be an instance of one of the subtypes.

- **Mutually Exclusive Rule:** This rule states that every entity instance of the super type can be an instance of only one entity subtype and not the other.

Drawing subtypes and supertypes: When drawing entity subtypes the following notes need to be kept in mind:

- Each subtype is a specialisation of a super type and therefore must be enclosed within an entity (see diagram).

- The common attributes and relationships for all subtypes must be listed in the super type only, but are inherited in every subtype.

- A subtype can and would generally have attributes and relationships of its own.

- There can never be just one subtype; another subtype should be created to cater for the rest (i.e. "OTHERS").

Implementation: There are two possible implementation routes:

- **If the subtypes contain attributes that are all the same:** If, by examining the data, it is clear that each of these entities share a common set of attributes, it becomes possible and very useful to amalgamate these subtypes into a new common super type entity called STAFF. So the data model with 5 separate entities is transformed into a single entity (table).

  What this means in practise is that, instead of defining 5 entities (tables), we only have to define one entity called STAFF, with an attribute which defines which subtype a particular instance (database record) belongs to and a second entity called STAFF TYPES which represents the legal STAFF subtypes.

  This is implemented so that all STAFF records are then stored in the same table. This table has a mandatory foreign key column called STAFF_TYPE and every new member of staff is thus "flagged", using this column to indicate which STAFF_TYPE they belong to. The STAFF_TYPE column is defined as a foreign key to a separate STAFF_TYPES table which thus contains a full compliment of the legal STAFF_TYPES.

  This is an important data model rationalisation because it means that a single common table can be used for looking for all staff, simply by adding a single "type" column to the table.

- **If the subtypes contain attributes which are different:** In this case each subtype will need to occupy its own table (entity) with its own particular definition. So for example, we could have the data for ADMIN STAFF occupying a completely different structure to the data for CLEANING STAFF. In this case we will create separate tables for each subtype, and define a separate foreign key to the subtype STAFF. The following procedure explains how to implement this:

- Step 1: Create a table for the super type with all common attributes and relationships.

- Step 2: Create a separate table for each subtype.

- Step 3: In the subtypes include the specific attributes and relationships.

- Step 4: Create a foreign key in the super type for each subtype.

- Step 5: Impose a constraint that only one foreign key may not be null (a super type MAY be associated to only one sub-type).

- Step 6: Impose a constraint that at least one foreign key must not be null (a super type MUST be associated to one sub-type).

3.5.5 Managing exclusive arcs

Exclusive Relationship Arc: There can be situations where an entity is either related to one entity or to another, but not to both. Whenever it is possible for a choice to be made between relationships, we define this using a so called exclusive relationship arc.

For example in the retail or manufacturing industry, a product can be either "bought-in" from another supplier or it can be manufactured "in-house". A product cannot be both; it must be one or the other. Thus, the relationship between an invoice line and the products it contains is somewhat complicated because there are actually 2 sets of products: *bought-in* products and *in-house* products. An invoice line can contain a product code from either set of products. This is modelled as follows, using the exclusive arc notation which is drawn across the affected relationships:

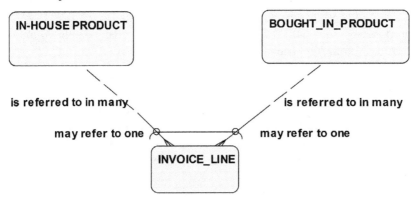

Rules of the exclusive relationship arc: The following rules need to be applied when drawing an exclusive relationship arc:

- A relationship arc may be applied to only one entity, called the target entity.

- The relationship arc must be applied to a minimum number of two relationships.

- The target entity will contain the foreign keys of the relationships affected by the arc.

- The optionality of the relationships affected by the arc must be the same from the perspective of the target entity.

- The optionality of the relationships affected by the arc may be different from the perspectives of the source entities.

- The relationships affected by the arc may have different cardinality (one-to-one, one-to-many).

Implementing an exclusive relationship arc: To implement an exclusive relationship arc, the following steps need to be taken:

- Step 1: Create a foreign key for each relationship affected by the arc. The foreign keys must be placed in the entity (table) to which the arc belongs.

- Step 2: Implement a constraint that allows only one foreign key value not to be null.

3.5.6 Managing non-Transferability of relationships: A relationship that is non-transferable will not allow the foreign key value to be updated, i.e. assigned to a different Parent Entity. For example, a typical example of a non-transferable relationship would be a Sales Order and Line Items relationship. Each particular Line Item can *only* be associated with one Sales Order throughout its entire life. If a Line Item is associated with the wrong sales order, it must be deleted and re-entered. It cannot be transferred to another sales order.

The non-transferable relationship is indicated visually on the Entity Relationship Diagram by a small diamond at the 'many' end of the relationship. Many relationships, however, are 'Transferable'. This means that the foreign key value *can* be assigned to another Parent Entity. For example, an Employee may be assigned to only one Department at a time, but is free to move from one Department to another over time.

Note the diamond notation at the non-transferable end of the order-lines relationship:

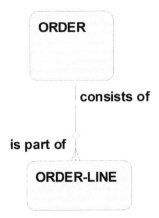

Implementation of Non-Transferability: When implementing the non-transferability of a relationship, a constraint is applied to the foreign key which does not allow the values to be updated.

3.5.7 Defining a Unique Identifier (UID): In a data model, one or more unique keys may be declared for each entity. Each unique key is composed from one or more data attributes of the entity. The set of unique keys declared for an entity is often referred to as the candidate keys for that entity. From the set of candidate keys, a single unique key is selected and declared the primary key for that entity.

There are four types of Unique Identifier (UID). When defining a UID for an entity, you will be defining a UID which is one of these types:

- Single Attribute UID

- Multiple Attribute UID

- Composed Attribute UID

- Composed Cascade Attribute UID

Below we will describe these types of Unique Identifiers and how they are defined and implemented.

3.5.7.1 Single Attribute UID: A single attribute UID is when an entity is made up of only one UID attribute which is not a foreign key.

E-R Diagram: Here the UID is the single attribute "ID" (indicated as a UID with the # sign):

```
EMPLOYEE
# ID
* FIRST NAME
* LAST NAME
o MOBILE NUMBER
* COMPANY CAR REG
```

Implementation: Primary Key is ID:

Table: Employees		
ID (the UID)	First Name	Last Name
1	John	Smith
2	Mary	Brown
3	Peter	Jones
4	Ann	Green

3.5.7.2 Multiple Attribute UID: A multiple UID attribute is when a primary key is made up of multiple attributes (composite primary key), all of which are non-foreign keys.

E-R Diagram: Here the UID is the double attribute combination of "NAME" and "VERSION". The combination is indicated as a UID with the # signs on the two attributes:

```
SOFTWARE
# NAME
# VERSION
* RELEASE DATE
o COMMENTS
```

Implementation: Primary Key is NAME and VERSION

Table: Software			
NAME (UID-1)	VERSION (UID-2)	Release Date	Comments
ORACLE	11g	01/12/2010	
SQL Server	2008	01/01/2008	MSoft
MySQL	5.2	15/06/2009	Oracle
MS Access	6	05/08/1994	

3.5.7.3 Composed Attribute UID: A composed attribute UID is when an entity has a primary key which is also a foreign key. These are marked with a UID Bar (the horizontal bar just above the crow's foot).

E-R Diagram: Here the UID of a RECIPE line is the composite of the UID of a Finished Product and the UID of a Raw Material. Note the bar across the two relationships - the so-called UID Bar.

UID Bar: In some cases (as in this example) a foreign key is *also* part of a primary key (UID), generally a composite key. Because Foreign Keys are *not* defined as attributes in a Logical data model, this creates a problem in defining the UID in the case where the UID is actually also a foreign key. This problem is solved in "Barker's Notation" using the UID bar. So, in our E-R diagram, the fact that the UID of RECIPE LINE is actually the composite of the foreign keys to the entities FINISHED PRODUCT and RAW MATERIAL is denoted using the UID Bar across both relationships, as follows:

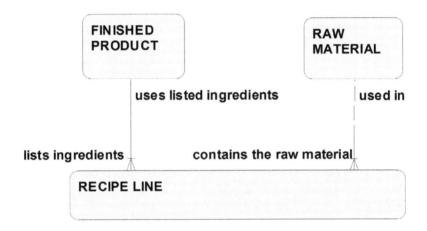

Implementation:

Table: Finished Product	
ID (UID)	**Finished Product**
1	Strawberry Jam
2	Tomato Chutney
3	Plum Jam

Table: Raw Material	
ID (UID)	Raw Material
1	Strawberries
2	Plums
3	Tomatoes
4	Sugar
5	Onions

The Primary Key (UID) of a Recipe Line is the composite of the Primary Keys of the Finished Product and each of its Raw materials:

Table: Recipe Lines	
Finished Product Id (UID 1)	Raw Material Id (UID 2)
1	1
1	4
2	3
2	4
2	5
3	2
3	4

3.5.7.4 Composed Cascade Attribute UID: A composed cascade UID attribute is when an entity uses its foreign keys as primary keys from an entity with composed (surrogate) UID attributes. A composed or surrogate UID is a UID which does not exist in nature. For example, an employee id, allocated when a new employee joins a company. It is an arbitrary unique number allocated to the employee. These artificial keys only gain importance when they are used to identify a real record.

In cases where there are parent-child relationships and parent entities have artificial / surrogate / composed keys, then we may find that child entities have UIDs entirely composed of a composite of these "unnatural" surrogate keys. Let's take an example:

Implementation:

Table: Hotels	
ID (UID)	Name
1	Holiday Inn
2	Hilton
3	Melia

A Hotel Id is a surrogate id for a Hotel.

Table: Floors	
Hotel Id	Floor Number
1	1
2	1
2	2

A Hotel Id (foreign key) and Floor Number are the UID for a floor in a hotel. Both are surrogate (artificial) keys.

Table: Rooms		
Hotel Id	Floor Number	Room Number
1	1	1
1	1	2
2	1	1
2	2	1
3	2	3

Here, Hotel Id (foreign key) and Floor Number (foreign key) and Room Number in ROOMS are the surrogate cascade attribute UID for a single room on one floor of a single hotel. This UID is entirely composed of surrogate (artificial keys).

---o0o---

4. Practical Logical Design using Oracle Designer

4.1 Employ a RAD approach: Oracle and its associated design tools (such as Oracle Designer) encourages a short-cycle prototyping approach rather than more traditional design methodologies with very long cycles of analysis, design, and development. Therefore, where possible we recommend the adoption of a so-called "RAD" approach. What is RAD exactly?

4.1.2 Rapid Application Development (RAD): This is a term originally used to describe a software development process introduced by James Martin, the Systems Design researcher, in 1991. RAD is a software development methodology which involves iterative design and development and the construction of prototypes. The basic principles of RAD are:

- Key objective is fast development and delivery of a high quality system with a relatively low investment.

- RAD aims to produce high quality systems quickly, primarily via iterative Prototyping, active user involvement, and computerized development tools. These tools may include GUI builders, Computer Aided Software Engineering (CASE) tools (in Oracle this would be Oracle Designer or a similar tool), Database Management Systems (DBMS), fourth-generation programming languages (in Oracle this may be PL/SQL), code generators (in Oracle this could be APEX, Oracle Forms, Reports, JDeveloper etc.) , and object-oriented techniques (in Oracle this would be the object-relational ability to embed code and validation properties in the database, associated with particular tables).

- Active user involvement is imperative. It generally includes a concept of joint application design (JAD), where users are intensely involved in system design, via structured workshops.

- Standard systems analysis and design methods can be fitted into a RAD framework.

- In RAD, the key emphasis is on fulfilling the business need, while technological or engineering excellence is of lesser importance.

- Project control involves prioritizing development and defining delivery deadlines or "timeboxes". If the project starts to slip, emphasis is on reducing requirements to fit the timebox, not in increasing the deadline. In a slipping schedule, non-essentials are abandoned.

- RAD attempts to reduce inherent project risk by breaking a project into smaller segments and providing more ease-of-change during the development process.

- RAD iteratively produces production software, as opposed to throwaway prototypes. Each RAD recursion is a working system. Each recursion seeks to come closer to the consensus of user requirements.

- RAD produces the documentation necessary to facilitate future development and maintenance.

4.1.3 The composition of the RAD team: Here is the typical makeup of a RAD team:

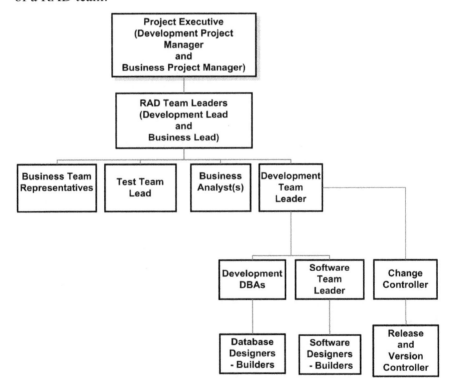

4.1.4 Setting up a RAD team: There are several key points in establishing a RAD Team:

- RAD can be seen as rather radical in some environments and therefore, setting up a RAD team needs to be done sensitively.

- The RAD team members need to understand the concept of RAD and the use of prototyping in iterative development.

- The core of the RAD methodology is the RAD review. A review is a meeting of the user and design and development group representatives to evaluate the latest RAD revision of the software. The review is "time-boxed" in that it is limited to a fixed amount of time, and takes place on strictly fixed dates. Slippage of dates of duration is unacceptable in the RAD methodology.

- The cycle of a RAD review should be as short as possible. A week (maximum 2 weeks) is usually considered an optimal cycle. This cycle is agreed at the beginning of the analysis and design phase and then it is rigorously applied to all RAD reviews.

- Each RAD cycle gives rise to a new version of the application. The content of a new version should be the changes evaluated and agreed at the last RAD review meeting. The exact content of a release should be gauged to allow time for changes to be made in between RAD reviews. Small releases are generally considered to be safer than large releases. It is easier to evaluate, agree and consolidate a small set of changes than a large one.

- RAD reviews must be rigorously minuted, documented and signed off by user and development team.

- The output from the RAD review will be a set of specific changes in database and software design, which is then passed to the team's Change Controller.

- The RAD methodology is maintained throughout Logical and Physical design-and-build phases of an application until final user acceptance.

4.2 Practical Steps in Logical Database Design using Oracle Designer

4.2.1 The preparatory stage:

- Create a new Application System in Designer.

- Define and identify business objectives, assumptions, critical success factors, key performance indicators and problems in Oracle Designer.

- Establish Business Direction Objectives in Oracle Designer.

- Ensure the development DBA is taking a copy of Oracle Designer repository at least once per day. This is where the team stores their work. Look after it and make sure the backups work and can be restored quickly.

4.2.2 The Analysis Stage: Using Oracle Designer to define a logical data model: The following are the key analyst steps to define the logical data model. The analyst works together with the business user to define the following data characteristics. These are then transferred to Oracle Designer by the business analyst using the E-R Diagrammer or the Repository Object Navigator:

- Identify business entities from users:

- Define the entities according to a defined naming standard for the application (singular name only for entities).

- Define basic E-R diagram (but no attributes) showing entities only:

- This initial E-R diagram should show entities grouped roughly by business area. This makes it more understandable for the business users in the RAD review team.

- Entities which are common to several business areas should be clustered in the middle of the diagram and available to all business areas.

- Identify and name relationships between entities:

- Establish relationships using a *Relationship matrix*. A relationship matrix is a matrix of entities versus entities. Together with the business users, it is possible to establish the existence of relationships between entities. Whenever a relationship of some kind is believed to exist, place a tick at the intersect of the 2 entities.

- Verify the relationships with each business area user.

- Name the relationships according to a defined standard for the application.

- Identify attributes for all entities:

- Together with the business users, identify the attributes that might be associated with each entity - ignore foreign keys for now (during logical design).

- Name the attributes according to a defined standard for the application (Keep attribute names simple and meaningful and not too long).

- Evaluate and define attribute optionality.

- Refine E-R diagram define cardinality / optionality of relationships:

- With each business area user, explore and define the optionality and cardinality of each relationship.

- Identify whether relationships are Identifying or Non-Identifying Relationships.

- An *identifying relationship* means a child entity cannot exist without a parent entity. The parent entity proves part of the key of the record of the child entity.

- In a *non-identifying relationship* a child entity can exist without an identifying parent entity. In other words, the parent entity does *not* provide a key to the child entity. Non-identifying relationships translate into foreign keys and these can be optional or mandatory - this translates into whether a foreign key in a physical database is optional or mandatory.

- Identify and define unique identifiers (UIDs) for all entities:

- Together with the business user, the analyst should identify the unique identifiers (UID) for each entity. There may be several for each entity. All must be defined.

- Determine which UID is going to be the primary UID. This will determine which columns will be used in the Primary Key constraint of the physical table definition at the physical design stage.

- Conclude all entities, attributes and relationship definitions including UIDs:

- Carry out final data model walkthroughs with the business users, explaining again the implications of the defined relationships, attributes and unique identifiers that have been identified. Conclude the user input to this phase of the logical design.

- Rationalise and normalise the data model:

- Resolve M:M Relationships

- Model Hierarchical Data

- Examine Recursive Relationships

- Model Exclusive Relationships

- Model Entity Type Hierarchies

- Finalise normalised data model.

- Hand over the data model to the physical database designers using DDT (database design transformer).

- Make any initial logical design changes originating from the physical designers.

4.2.3 Using Oracle Designer together with RAD Design reviews: Oracle Designer (or a similar tool) is ideal for defining and illustrating the business entities and their relationships, together with the business users in a series of RAD reviews. Here is how the Designer tool should be used in this context:

- **The ERD tool:** Use the *Entity Relationship Diagrammer* (ERD) tool initially until basic E-R diagram, entities and relationships are initially defined and agreed with the business users.

- **Start Modelling with the business user:** Use this E-R diagram as the initial starting point for a RAD design (as a RAD discussion document) with the business users.

- **Consolidate the data model:** During some RAD reviews, refine and agree this basic E-R diagram and model as the process progresses. Consolidate the data model in small, steady steps.

- **Collect Attributes and UIDs:** When the basic E-R definition is agreed by the business users and business analysts, then use the *Repository Object Navigator* (RON) to start to collect detailed attribute and UID information.

- **Present E-R Diagrams in RAD reviews:** Use Entity Relationship Diagrammer (ERD) to provide the user with constantly upgraded versions of the data model as attributes and UIDs are added.

- **Create "Sub Views":** In large systems it is wise to break the E-R diagrams into "sub views" of the data model, which are the business areas that are relevant to a particular business user group; otherwise the total system can appear overwhelmingly complex for a normal business user and therefore less useful as the basis of the RAD review. As a rule of thumb a business area is unlikely to include more than 50 basic entities in total, whereas a total system may include several hundred, most of which are irrelevant to a particular business user.

- **Normalization and Rationalisation:** When the basic E-R data model is concluded, use the Repository Object Navigator (RON) and Entity Relationship Diagrammer to carry out and complete normalization to 3rd normal form and any appropriate data rationalisation. During the RAD reviews, explain to the business users why this is important and how it affects the data model.

- **Supplement ERD with useful information:** Populate the logical data model with additional information using the Repository Object Navigator (RON). Additional information includes: Attribute properties, Entity properties, Relationship properties, Synonyms, etc.

- **Forward Engineer to Physical Design Stage:** When the data model passes the "Pre-Transformation Checklist" (see later), it is ready to be forward engineered into a physical server data model. This is done together with the Design DBA, using the Database Design Transformer (DDT) in Oracle Designer.

- **Note:** Obviously logical design definitions can be *manually* transferred to a physical design repository in Oracle Designer or another Designer tool, but this causes a huge repetition of work and is not an optimal strategy. Using the DDT or a similar utility is the preferred route.

---oOo---

5. Moving from the Logical to the Physical design

5.1 Moving forward from Logical to Physical Design in Designer: Having completed the logical design, and the data model normalization and rationalisation, it is now time to move on to creating the physical database design. This is the last step prior to building the physical database itself.

5.2 Database Design Transformer: Oracle Designer provides an automated route from the Logical data model to the Physical Database design, using its *Database Design Transformer*. This utility is an essential part of transforming a logical data model to a physical design. The alternative is the manual entry of the entire physical design again into Oracle Designer.

5.2.1 Advice: The *Database Design Transformer* (DDT) can be used iteratively, which means you can build your first-pass Physical database design, check that it is correct and then alter and correct the original Logical data model for errors or omissions, then rebuild the Physical database design. This recursive process can be repeated endlessly - but generally a moment will come when you think that the Logical data model is correct and complete. At this point, further changes and maintenance to the Logical model can cease.

Here is the basic Design transformation process flow:

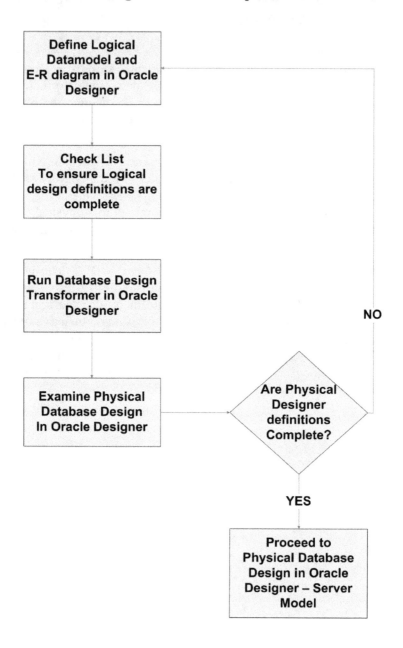

5.2.2 Getting the most out of the Database Design Transformer:
There are a few issues which should be understood when generating the
Physical Database design using the DDT utility in Oracle Designer:

- **Remember there will be post-transformation actions:** Modifications to the physical model will *always* be necessary after the DDT has executed. For example, if the application requires server-derived columns such as sequence numbers and date stamps (which most do), this can *only* be specified *after* the DDT has executed: in other words, at the physical level against specific database columns.

So it is important to realise that the physical database design that is generated by the DDT will *not* be the final product. There will still be quite a lot of physical Database design work to do after the transformations have been completed.

- **Pre-Transformation:** Get the most out of the Logical Data model definitions. The *Database Design Transformer* is a very sophisticated utility that builds Physical database definitions, based on the Logical definitions you entered for your data model.

Because, the DDT uses virtually every piece of information you enter in the E-R definitions to generate the Physical model, it is crucial, therefore, to thoroughly describe the Entity Model *before* the utility is run. This will save the analyst time when development moves to the design stage and in cases where modules for screens and reports are also being created in Designer.

Below is a checklist of the areas an analyst should examine before running the DDT. The savvy reader may note that many of the areas described below can also be specified in the physical model *after* the DDT has executed. While this is true, the purpose of the DDT is to transform the logical model into a physical model, using the information that has been collected and entered at this point. The advantage of specifying the information now, is that the DDT will automatically populate areas in the physical model, thus saving the designer much time and effort later. So don't skimp on these tasks, otherwise you will regret it when it comes to the physical database definition stage.

5.2.3 Pre-Transformation Checklist: Use this checklist on your logical design before carrying out the transformation to a physical design:

5.2.3.1. Domains: If Domains are being used, make sure to execute the 'Update Attributes in Domain' utility *before* running the DDT. Certain modifications made to a domain after it has been assigned to an attribute, are *not* automatically inherited by attributes that use that domain (DEFAULT value, for example). Domains are used by the application generators for defining valid value constraints: for example, a pop-list containing a finite list of values. In addition, Domains are used to enforce standard definitions among common attributes in different entities, e.g. all LAST NAME attributes are defined as VARCHAR2 with a length of 30. Also, if Check Constraints have not been explicitly defined during the Design Stage, the SQL DDL Generator can use Domains to generate Check Constraints, provided the 'Valid value constraints' checkbox in 'Options' tab is checked.

5.2.3.2. Check UIDs: Check the Unique Identifier (UID) definitions in the entities. Ensure that when a foreign key relationship forms part of the Primary Key, that the relationship is included in the UID definition for the entity. A classic example is a parent-child relationship in which a 'one-to-many' relationship exists between the two entities. When the relationship forms part of the Unique Identifier (and you have included this relationship in the UID Definition), this will be visually represented in the Entity Relationship Diagram by a line drawn at the base of the "crow's foot" at the 'many' side of the relationship. If a UID is not specified for an entity, the DDT will automatically create one (with an associated Oracle sequence).

5.2.3.3. Do not record Foreign Keys: Do not record Foreign Key Relationships as attributes in the related entity. This is a departure from other modelling tools such as Erwin, in which foreign key columns *do* appear on the Entity Relationship Diagram. The DDT will create foreign key columns in those entities at the 'many' end of the relationship. If the foreign key is specified as an attribute of an entity which *also* has a foreign key relationship defined for it, then the foreign key column will be duplicated. Also be sure to scrutinize the 'Optionality' of the relationship at the 'many' end of the entity. The optionality indicates whether the columns that migrate to the foreign key table, i.e., the 'many' end of the relationship, are optional or mandatory.

5.2.3.4. Transferable: Inspect the 'Transferable' checkbox of the relationships (the default is checked). A relationship that is non-transferable will not allow the foreign key valued to be updated, i.e. assigned to a different Parent Entity. A typical example of a non-transferable relationship would be a Sales Order and Line Items relationship. Each particular Line Item can *only* be associated with one Sales Order throughout its entire life. The non-transferable relationship will be indicated visually on the Entity Relationship Diagram by a small diamond at the 'many' end of the relationship. Many relationships, however, are 'Transferable'. This means that the foreign key value *can* be assigned to another Parent Entity. For example, an Employee may be assigned to only one Department at a time, but is free to move from one Department to another over time.

5.2.3.5. Plurals and Short Names: Check the Plurals and Short Names for Entities. The Plurals will become the table names (Table names are always plural - entities are always singular) and Designer will automatically generate Plurals and Short Names for Entities if they're not specified. Even though it does a good job of making Entities plural (even those ending in 's'), it's a good idea to check them over thoroughly. Also check the Short Names generated by Designer/2000. The Short Names will be used for aliases in SELECT statements in the generated application. If the names that Designer generated are not satisfactory, change them here.

5.2.3.6. Foreign Key Columns - generated names: By default, both the Database Design Wizard and the Database Design Transformer will prefix foreign key columns with the entity name from which they migrated. This can result in long, undesirable column names for foreign key columns. In the Options tab of the DDT, make sure that the 'Prefix Foreign key columns' checkbox and the 'Prefix surrogate key columns' checkbox in the 'Naming Conventions' area are not checked.

5.2.3.7. Constraint Implementation: In the Options tab of the DDT, check that the 'Constraint implementation level' is set to "Both" and not just "Client" or "Server". Do this if you want to generate application logic in addition to database logic for Primary and Foreign key constraints. By specifying "Both", validation logic for enforcement of constraints will be created in both the client application (if you are planning to generate it from Designer) and in the database. You won't see the result of this option in the database design itself, but rather in the generated application code. For example, in Oracle Forms, WHEN-VALIDATE-ITEM triggers will be generated to enforce constraints at the client. For Oracle Webserver, client-side Javascript code will be generated.

5.2.3.8. Default Values: If attributes have Default Values, be sure to specify them either in the Domain or directly to the attribute. Default Values will be implemented in the SQL DDL, e.g., COLUMN1, VARCHAR2(3), DEFAULT 'ZZZ'. Although Default Values are intended to store fixed values, Designer will recognize SYSDATE for the Default Value. In addition, the application generators use Default Values to insert default values into form fields.

5.2.3.9. Volume definitions: Specify Volume characteristics, in particular the number of Start Rows and End Rows. These will be used to determine sizing estimates for use with the 'Database Table and Index Sizing' Repository Report. For those rows where an End value is not known or cannot be estimated, you can specify the 'Average Growth'. Even though this field is not used by the 'Database Table and Index Sizing' Repository Report, it is useful documentation for the DBA in sizing the Tables and Indexes.

5.2.3.10. Entity Descriptions: Thoroughly describe entities with descriptions. Descriptions, by default, will be transformed into the 'User Help Text' Table property in the database design. This property is used by the application generators to create context-sensitive online help, so be sure to make it meaningful to end users. The Notes field provides an additional place to describe an entity or include technical notes for developers; however, this field is not used by the application generators.

5.2.3.11. Attribute Descriptions: Describe the attributes with descriptions and comments. Descriptions, by default, will be transformed into the 'User Help Text' Column property in the database design. As with entities, this property is used by the application generators to generate context-sensitive online help, so again, be sure to make it meaningful to end users. Comments will be used for item level Hint Text in generated applications, so be sure to make the Comment meaningful and short (less than one line). In addition, the SQL DDL generator will use "Comments" for column comments in the database. The Notes field provides an additional place to describe an attribute or include technical notes for developers; however, this field is not used by the application generators.

5.3 Checking the Generated Physical Design: Before leaving the Design Transformer and moving on to the physical database design itself, use the checklist above to ensure that you no longer need to use the Database Design Transformer. This is a very important decision, for the following reason:

Once you start editing the physical database design itself, you cannot use the DDT again to generate a physical design for this application system, otherwise you will certainly over-write the edits you have made in the physical design editor. Therefore, before proceeding to the physical design, please be absolutely sure you have finished with the logical design and the design transformer tool.

5.4 A general comment about keeping a Designer backup: Keeping a backup of the Oracle Designer repository is vital during all phases of design and development. In a large development, the loss of even a single day's work could be an expensive mistake. It is also important to take separate backups at key moments in the project life-cycle. These include the moment when logical design (Analysis) is completed and physical design begins.

---o0o---

6. Practical Physical Design using Oracle Designer

6.1 Introduction to Physical Database Design: An experienced designer in a "well-understood" business environment can enter the database design process at this point, and thus avoid the Logical design phase. In either case, at some moment we will arrive at the point of carrying out the physical database design. Let us see what this means in practice.

6.1.1 Physical Design: During the logical design phase, we defined a data model consisting of entities, attributes, and relationships. The entities are linked together using relationships. Attributes are used to describe the entities. The unique identifier (UID) distinguishes between one instance of an entity and another.

During the physical design process, we translate the schemas into actual database structures, mapping:

- Entities to tables
- Relationships to foreign key constraints
- Attributes to columns
- Primary unique identifiers to primary key constraints
- Unique identifiers to unique key constraints

6.1.2 Physical Design Structures: Once we have converted the logical design to a physical one using the Data Design Transformer, we must then define and create some (or all) of the following physical data structures:

- Tablespaces
- Tables and Partitioned Tables
- Views
- Integrity Constraints

Some of these structures require disk space. Others exist only in the data dictionary, like constraints to guarantee data integrity. The following structures may be created to improve performance:

- Indexes and Partitioned Indexes

- Materialized Views

6.1.3 An Explanation of Oracle Physical Structures: Here is a brief explanation of the physical data structures which need to be defined. If you are using the Database Design Transformer, many of these database objects will already have been created. If not, then all of these objects will need to be defined.

Some of these objects (tablespaces etc.) need to be defined by a Development DBA with experience of sizing production systems.

6.1.3.1 Tablespaces: A tablespace consists of one or more datafiles, which are physical structures within the operating system you are using. A datafile is associated with only one tablespace. From a design perspective, tablespaces are containers for physical design structures, like tables and indexes.

When defining tablespaces, it is important for the Development DBA to remember that they need to be separated according to their use:

- Tablespaces containing tables should be separated from tablespaces containing their indexes.

- Small tables should be in different tablespaces to large tables.

- Tablespaces should also represent logical business units, if possible. Therefore, because a tablespace is the coarsest granularity for backup and recovery, the logical business design also affects availability and maintenance.

6.1.3.2 Tables: Tables are the basic unit of data storage. In relational databases a table is a set of data elements that is organized using a model of vertical columns (identified by a column name) and horizontal rows of data. A table has a *specified* number of columns, but can have *any number of rows*. Each row is identified by the values appearing in a particular group of columns which are identified as a unique key (UID).

6.1.3.3 Partitioned Tables: Using partitioned tables instead of non-partitioned ones addresses a key problem of supporting very large data volumes. It allows the developer to divide very large tables into smaller and more manageable pieces.

The main design criterion for partitioning is manageability, though there are also performance benefits in most cases. For example, we might choose a partitioning strategy based on the month of a transaction date. If the database contains many years of data, the use of monthly partitioned tables reduces the query size to a much smaller data set and therefore will return a much faster response.

6.1.3.4 Views: A view is a tailored presentation of the data contained in one or more tables (or other views). A view takes the output of a pre-defined query and treats it as if it was a table. Views do not require any space in the database. The data in a view does not have to be physically stored in the database. In queries, a view behaves like a normal Oracle table, but the view's data are "calculated" at query time, rather than being physically stored in the database.

6.1.3.5 Constraints (database constraints): Constraints are rules of *data integrity* for a database that limit the acceptable data values for a table. They are the optional schema objects that depend on a table. The existence of a table without any constraint is possible, but the existence of a constraint without any table is not possible.

Constraints generally enforce business rules in a database. If a constraint is violated during a transaction, the transaction will fail, be rolled-back and a specific error occurs.

Constraints can be created along with the table in the CREATE TABLE statement. Addition and deletion of constraints can be done in the ALTER TABLE statement. The following types of constraints are available in Oracle Database:

- **NOT NULL:** It enforces that a column, declared as not null, cannot have any NULL values. For example, if an employee's hire date is not known, then that employee may not be considered as a valid employee.

- **UNIQUE:** It ensures that columns protected by this constraint, cannot have duplicate values.

- **PRIMARY KEY:** It is responsible for uniquely identifying a row in a table. A table can have only one PRIMARY KEY constraint. A PRIMARY KEY constraint completely includes both the NOT NULL and UNIQUE constraints. It is enforced with an index on all columns in the key.

- **FOREIGN KEY:** It is also known as referential integrity constraint. It enforces that values referenced in one table are defined in another table. It establishes a parent-child or reference-dependent relationship between the two tables.

- **CHECK:** It enforces that columns must meet a specific condition that is evaluated to a Boolean value. If the value evaluates to false, then the database will raise an exception, and not allow the INSERT and UPDATE statements to operate on columns.

6.1.3.6 Indexes: An Index is an Oracle database object associated with a table. Indexes provide improved access to table rows by storing sorted values from specific columns and using those sorted values to find associated table rows more easily. This means that data can be found without having to look at more than a fraction of the total rows within a table. Indexes are optional, but generally associated with primary and unique keys and often with foreign key columns.

The use of indexes is not always positive. An index may improve data retrieval speed, but inserting data is less efficient, because every new record means that one or more indexes need to be updated. This reduces performance and this can be a disadvantage for OLTP database processing. However, in a data warehouse environment (where transaction processing doesn't happen) indexes can be used without too much consideration and generally yield performance improvements.

Indexes occupy space and must be defined within a tablespace and have a full logical and physical storage definition.

Indexes in Data warehousing: In addition to the classical B-tree indexes, bitmap indexes are common in data warehousing environments. Bitmap indexes are optimized index structures for set-oriented operations. Additionally, they are necessary for some optimized data access methods such as star transformations.

6.1.3.7 Partitioned Indexes: Indexes are just like tables in that you can also partition them. The partitioning strategy is not dependent upon the table structure. Partitioning indexes may improve query performance.

6.1.3.8 Materialized Views: Materialized views are query results that have been stored in advance, so that long-running calculations are not necessary when SQL select statements are executed. From a physical design point of view, materialized views resemble tables. Materialized views can improve performance, especially in data warehouse environments with very large base data volumes.

6.1.3.9 Sequences: In Oracle, you can create auto numbering by defining and using a Sequence. A sequence is an object in Oracle that is used to generate the next unique number. This can be useful when you need to create a unique number to act as a primary key. To use a particular sequence, first define the sequence in Oracle Designer. Then refer to the new sequence in the appropriate column definition of the

Design editor. Generally Sequences are named in some logical way, usually with a form such as TABLE_NAME_SEQ.

6.1.3.10 Using Designer Domains: In Oracle Designer, a domain defines a set of validation rules, format constraints and other properties that apply to a group of entity attributes, columns, program data constructs, module arguments, data structure items or unbound items. For example, a designer may define a domain called "Boolean" to contain the values "Y", or "N" for "Yes" and "No". This domain can then be associated with a Column definition in Designer.

If you make a change to a domain, you can propagate the updates to associated columns or attributes using the Update Columns in a Domain or Update Attributes in a Domain utility, available from the Utilities menu on the Repository Object Navigator of Designer.

Domains are useful because they save the designer from having to define the same database constraint / validation rules repeatedly. For example, there are often many "flag columns" in a typical database which only permit a Boolean entry. This would be implemented by creating a "BOOLEAN" domain in Oracle Designer, with 2 entries: "Y" meaning "Yes" and "N" meaning "No". These domains are implemented from Designer by using a physical database Check constraint or by generating a separate domain table usually called CG_REF_CODES against which related columns are validated.

Advice: Domains should only be used for data validation where the data is absolutely static, i.e. where there is absolutely no possibility of new values being added or old values changed or deleted. A Boolean domain is a good example of this.

6.1.3.11 Database Triggers: A database trigger is procedural code that is automatically executed in response to certain events in a schema. The most often used triggers are those that are based on transactions against a particular table or view in a database - so called DML Triggers. However, other types of Schema Triggers exist which execute when DDL commands are executed (CREATE, DROP, ALTER) and also before and after user login and logout.

DML Triggers: An Oracle table can have a number of database triggers associated with it. These triggers contain and execute PL/SQL code when a particular DML event occurs on that table, such as an INSERT, UPDATE or DELETE.

Triggers are defined in Oracle Designer as part of the table definition and they are generated together with the table when the physical database is built.

Triggers are useful for all kinds of reasons. For example, a trigger can be used to generate a new Primary key from an Oracle Sequence when a new record is INSERTed into to a table. A trigger can be used to cascade an update to one or more other tables. Triggers are often used to write records of transactions into auditing tables, for instance, where it is necessary to produce complete audit trails of transactional activity.

Triggers operate as part of an existing DML transaction and they work on an "All or Nothing" basis. So, triggers are very safe, because if the underlying transaction fails, the trigger is rolled back and also, if a trigger fails, the underlying transaction is rolled back. Therefore, either an entire transaction is committed (including the trigger) or none of it is committed.

The four main types of triggers are:

- Row Level Trigger: This gets executed before or after *any column value of a row* changes.

- Column Level Trigger: This gets executed before or after the *specified column* changes.

- For Each Row Type: This trigger gets executed once for each row of the result set caused by insert/update/delete.

- For Each Statement Type: This trigger gets executed only once for the entire result set, but fires each time the statement is executed.

Mutating tables: When a single SQL statement modifies several rows of a table at once, the order of the operations is not well-defined; there is no "order by" clause on "update" statements, for example. Row-level triggers are executed as each row is modified, so the order in which trigger code is run is also not well-defined. Oracle protects the programmer from this uncertainty by preventing row-level triggers from modifying other rows in the *same table*. This is the "mutating table" phenomenon mentioned in the error message which Oracle produces if you attempt this. One solution to the risk of table mutation is to have row-level triggers place information into a temporary table, indicating what further changes need to be made, and then have a statement-level trigger fire just once, at the end, to perform the requested changes and clean up the temporary table.

Because a foreign key's referential actions are implemented via implied triggers, they are similarly restricted. This may become a problem when defining a self-referential foreign key, or a cyclical set of such constraints, or some other combination of triggers and CASCADE rules. For example, if a user deletes a record from table A, CASCADE rule on table A deletes a record from table B, and a trigger on table B attempts to SELECT from table A, a Mutating table error will occur.

6.1.3.12 Database Stored Procedures: A stored procedure is a PL/SQL (or Java) program stored in the Oracle database. Typical uses for stored procedures include data validation integrated within the database or access control mechanisms. Stored procedures can consolidate and centralise logic within the database. Extensive or complex processing that requires execution of several SQL statements can be placed into these stored procedures, and then called by any number of external applications or database triggers. One can use nested stored procedures by executing one stored procedure from within another. This centralisation of executable code reduces code repetition and maintenance costs.

Stored procedures are similar to user-defined functions. The main difference is that functions can be used like any other expression within a SQL statement, whereas stored procedures must be invoked. Program control passes temporarily to the called procedure.

6.1.3.13 User Defined Functions: A function is a named program unit that takes parameters and returns a computed value. For instance, in SQL there are many built-in, pre-defined functions like MAX, COUNT, LOG etc. These functions work by being passed values and then returning a result, for example:

SELECT COUNT(NAME) from EMP;

In addition to all the pre-defined functions which already exist in Oracle, it is possible for the designer to define and create completely new functions which are highly specific to a particular application. These functions might convert data values or evaluate user data access rights, or any number of other possible applications. They may also be in constant use and for this reason a User-defined Function can be stored in the database and called by any number of users. The definition of a User-defined function is made in Oracle designer, and generated into a physical database during the "Build phase" of a development in the same way as other database objects.

6.1.3.14 Storage Definitions: During the physical design process, the issue of physical database storage arises. There are several stages in the process of storage allocation. In Designer it is possible to define a named set of storage parameters for use in the SQL STORAGE clause. These parameters affect both the time taken to access data and how efficiently space is used. The allocated storage minimizes the frequency with which objects are allocated additional space. The storage details defined here can subsequently be associated with other database object definitions (e.g., tablespaces, rollback segments, tables, etc.). In Designer, this is defined using the Repository Object Navigator under Storage Definitions.

Tablespaces and Tables: A set of Tablespaces should be defined together with the Development DBA. The number of tablespaces depends on the application and their intended use, e.g. for Indexes or for different types of Tables (transactional, referential etc.), or split by business area etc. These are design decisions which are impacted by both performance and housekeeping considerations.

Simultaneously, storage definitions also need to be defined which will match the target production environment. Again, the definitions of storage clauses is determined by many issues such as data growth rates, The defined storage clauses should then be associated with the appropriate tablespace definitions.

Finally, the tables and indexes in the physical model need to be associated with specific tablespaces. This is defined in Oracle Designer using the Repository Object Navigator under Oracle databases / Storage / Tablespaces / Storing Tables / Indexes / Partitions etc.

Here is a simplified guide to defining and building the database administration objects during physical design and database build:

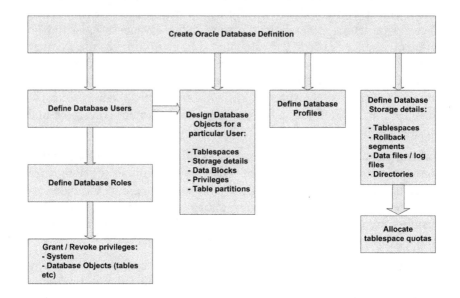

6.2 Practical steps in completing the Physical Database Design: After converting the Logical data model into a Physical Server model in Oracle Designer, the following steps are necessary to complete the design and build a physical database:

Step 1: Analyze and Refine the Relational Model and add missing physical object definitions in Oracle Designer:

- Modify table properties according to requirements (partitions etc).

- Discover and define missing constraints (domains etc.).

- Discover missing foreign keys and define.

- Define indexes.

- Define tablespaces / storage / volume properties.

- Define views.

- Define Materialized Views.

- Define stored procedures.

- Define user-defined functions.

- Define database triggers.
- Define object synonym definitions (tables and views).

Step 2: Add additional definitions for tables and views:

- This includes user interface definitions like Prompts, Help, alignment, uppercase etc. This is especially important if Designer is to be used to generate application code.
- Define roles, users and assign users to roles.
- Define grants for roles to tables and views.

Step 3: Generate the database DDL:

- Use Designer to generate DDL for your Database.
- Execute the DDL script into a target database instance.
- Validating the physical database against the Oracle designer definitions.

Step 4: Recursion: Rebuilding a database from an altered design:

- When to regress to the logical data model?
- Comparing the Relational Model Changes with what is in the Database.
- Reviewing and Making Changes to the physical data model .
- Forward Engineering to a New Relational Model.
- Synchronizing the Data Dictionary with Changes in a Model.

We will deal with Step 3 and Step 4 in later chapters.

---o0o---

7. Designing a database for Performance

Performance of an Oracle database is dependent on many factors, including system architecture, system and Oracle configuration, database design, software design, and system maintenance. Here we provide a basic introduction to just the database design issues which affect the performance of an Oracle database. A later volume deals with this subject in much more comprehensive detail and addresses all the other issues which affect performance.

7.1 What do we mean by Oracle database performance? The word performance relates to the ability of the database to deliver data or transactions at a rate which is considered to be adequate or better than adequate to meet the requirements of the business.

Thus, performance can be something of a moveable feast. An online transaction taking 30 seconds may be considered as not performing well, whereas an overnight daily batch job taking 15 minutes may be considered to be performing very well. It just depends on the expectation and on the business constraints.

7.2 Setting performance parameters for each part of a system: Because of the subjective nature of performance and the context in which performance is judged, it is good practice to define a set of "System Performance Standards" during system, database and functional design. This document should contain a detailed statement of the functional elements of the system (including transactions, queries, batch jobs, and housekeeping activities) and for each functional element a minimum and maximum performance standard should be allocated. Obviously, these standards will depend entirely on the context of the function. A daily batch job which takes 30 hours would clearly be unacceptable, but equally when batch activities are chained together in daily batch jobs, the performance of each may very quickly become very critical.

The performance standards should look something like this example:

Function Id	Freq	Max Concurrency	Max cycle (secs)	OLTP / BATCH
BIOTR001	24000/day	100 user	30 secs	OLTP
BIOBA023	2/day	1 user	900 secs	BATCH
BIOTR007	1200/day	8 user	30 secs	OLTP

7.3 What database design issues affect Oracle performance? It is an unfortunate reality that most Oracle development and production teams spend more time dealing with performance problems *after* an application goes into in production than during its design phase.

This is despite the fact that it is usually the architecture and design of an application that limits its ultimate performance potential. A hasty design decision made early in the application's lifecycle can require days or months of corrective action, once the application is deployed.

So what are the specific database design strategies that can affect how well a database performs in production?

- De-normalization.

- Predefined optimal views.

- Index Design.

- Table and Index Partitioning.

- Table compression.

- Materialized views.

- Parallel execution.

7.4 What specific steps can we take to design-in good database performance? The following provides details of the specific actions necessary to ensure that the database design will permit good performance:

7.4.1 De-normalization: In an OLTP application, the design objective is a data model of 3rd normal form. Generally speaking, this objective should never be ignored, because denormalized databases create risks of data and functional redundancy.

However, in reality, there are many cases where the performance benefits outweigh the "redundancy" costs of de-normalization. Very often, when an application often needs to access summary data from "child records", for example where an order header needs to contain the sum of the values of the order lines (perhaps to calculate order discount levels). It may be that there is a case to pre-calculate this summary data whenever child records are changed.

The additional processing time to summarise child records occurs just once per update, whereas a request for the summed data may occur many thousands of times in a transaction life-cycle. The design decision to denormalize summary data is thus totally dependent on the case in hand and the business requirement for denormalized summary data. A similar decision exists in the case of many other types of "derived" data which can also be denormalized into the production database.

7.4.2 Predefined optimal views: Firstly, creating a view may make a final SQL query simpler, but it doesn't alter the underlying query that is executed. A view based on a complex, de-optimal query will be complex and de-optimal every time the view is queried, so do not imagine that a view will improve performance simply because the view is more simple to query than the underlying tables.

However, a view can be pre-defined to be an optimal query. For example, a query which involves several table joins can be defined in a view in a way which is optimal. This optimised view can then be defined and used in an application. The definition of a view that includes an *optimised* query can be useful, because it reduces the risk of a user issuing a de-optimal, poorly performing query.

7.4.3 Index Design: As we have seen, indexes are meant to improve read efficiency of a SQL query. We have also seen that they do this at the expense of write efficiency. This means that having an index will slow down inserts but may well speed up select (and update and delete) statements.

Whilst the addition of an index to a table always slows down insert statements, it doesn't always follow that an index will *always* speed up select statements. For example, an index that is ignored during execution of a SQL select statement is just a liability. Also, in general, indexes improve performance on *large* tables, but on *small* tables it is often better to read the whole table (full-table scan) rather than using an index. Again, for *small* tables, indexes are often a liability, especially if the table is read many times by an application. In such a case, reading an index *and* a table for a very small table is a waste of I/O resources, and will damage performance.

We can see from these considerations that indexes need to be carefully designed to ensure that they actually provide a real benefit.

Basic indexes: Basic index design calls for the existence of an index on the following columns:

- Primary key column(s) - Unique index

- Unique key column(s) - Unique index

- Foreign key column(s) - Non-unique index

Application specific indexes: In addition to these basic indexes a database designer may wish to create specific indexes on other columns which are used as follows:

- Columns frequently used in queries - Non-unique index

- Columns frequently used in queries with a function - Function index

Testing index efficiency: When Oracle executes a SQL statement, it determines the optimal access path to the data by means of the Oracle Optimizer. The purpose of the Oracle Optimizer is to determine the most efficient execution plan for your queries. It makes these decisions based on the statistical information it has about the data and by leveraging Oracle database features such as hash joins, parallel query, partitioning, etc. Still, it is expected that the optimizer will generate sub-optimal plans for some SQL statements in some circumstances. In these cases, the first step in diagnosing why the SQL "Optimizer" has picked a sub-optimal plan is to visually inspect the execution plan.

Optimizer and EXPLAIN PLAN: There are many tools available to show the execution plan being used for a SQL statement. SQL*Developer, Enterprise Manager and Toad, all provide a GUI representation and some analysis of the execution plan of a particular SQL statement. Provided the tests are being conducted in a production-size database, much useful design information can be gleaned from the results of these analyses. The basic questions in terms of Index design in conjunction with a particular SQL statement are:

- Is an optimal access path being used to retrieve the data?

- Would an index improve the access path and therefore improve performance?

- If so, what columns should the index include?

- When creating an index, remember that indexes are not always good all the time. Sometimes an index may be useful and sometimes it may be better to disable the index for a particular query.

7.4.4 Using Optimizer hints in stored procedures to improve performance: Because there are times when an index should be used and times when it should not be used, Oracle provides a way of guiding the Optimizer's actions. This is done by embedding a series of "hints" into the SQL code.

These hints can also be applied to SQL code which is designed and embedded in stored database procedures. These "hints" apply not only to index usage but also to other execution path decisions of the SQL Optimizer. There are many possible hints and their use is well-documented in Oracle white papers. When defining stored procedures / triggers, do remember to performance optimise these procedures in the same way as non-database-stored procedural code.

7.4.5 Table Partitioning: Using partitioned tables instead of non-partitioned ones addresses a key problem of supporting very large data volumes. It allows the developer to divide very large tables into smaller and more manageable pieces. Partitioning a table is a design decision. For example, we may have a very large table containing invoices and invoice lines. It would seem logical to partition invoices (and invoice lines) by month or week number. However, in reality, a business may be highly seasonal and so partitioning these tables would give rise to some very large partitions and some small or empty partitions. Thus, a design decision needs to be made when considering partitioned tables. In this example, it may be more rational to define a partition according to YEAR and CUSTOMER_NAME or define some other partition key like Trimester.

7.4.6 Table compression: You can save disk space, increase memory efficiency, and improve query performance by compressing heap-organized tables. This often leads to better scalability and query performance. You can enable compression at the tablespace, table, or partition level. Partitioned tables are a good candidate for table compression. Although compressed tables or partitions are updatable, there is some overhead in updating these tables, and high update activity may work against compression by causing some space to be wasted.

OLTP table compression is best suited for tables with significant update activity. Hybrid Columnar Compression, a feature of certain Oracle storage systems, utilizes a combination of both row and columnar methods for storing data. When data is loaded, groups of rows are stored in columnar format, with the values for a given column stored and compressed together. Storing column data together, with the same data type and similar characteristics, drastically increases the storage savings achieved from compression. Hybrid Columnar Compression provides multiple levels of compression and is best suited for tables or partitions with minimal update activity.

7.4.7 Materialized views: Materialized views are query results that have been stored in advance so that long-running calculations are not necessary when SQL select statements are executed. From a physical design point of view, materialized views resemble tables. Materialized views can improve performance, especially in data warehouse environments with very large base data volumes.

7.4.8 Locking issues: Although record locking is properly an issue which concerns functional design, it does impact on design of stored procedures and database triggers. There are several issues that have to be kept in mind when designing DML code for triggers and procedures:

- **Lock contention** - this causes one process to wait for one or more records to be released from existing row level locks taken by another process. Contention can cause processing delays.

- **Deadlocking** - this phenomenon occurs when 2 processes attempt to lock the same sets of records but in the opposite order. Process 1 locks some records in Table A and then attempts to lock some records in Table B. Process 2 has already locked these same records in Table B (causing process 1 to wait) and is attempting to lock the same records in Table A, but is forced to wait because process 1 has already locked the records. Both processes are forced to wait - basically forever. Such "deadlocks" are automatically detected and cause a rollback and error by the detecting process.

To avoid these 2 problems, the following design strategies should be adopted when scripting PL/SQL statements in procedures and triggers:

- Lock records late and commit early: This means take record locks as late as possible in a procedure and execute a commit statement as soon as it is functionally safe to do so. This rule ensures that records are locked for the minimum amount of time. For example, it is unwise and often unnecessary, to issue a locking statement such as the following at the beginning of a long running procedure:

SELECT ..... FOR UPDATE....

This locks a record set until it encounters a commit or rollback statement. If the processing that follows such a statement is relatively time-consuming, it could be that locked records begin to cause locking contention for other processes trying to lock these records. Using explicit PL/SQL cursors can avoid the need to lock large numbers of records for a long time.

- Always lock tables in the same order in all processes. This discipline avoids the risk of dead-locking, because all processes will always attempt to lock in the same order. The rule for the order in which processes lock tables needs to be agreed and established at a project level, so that it is universally adopted by designers and programmers.

---oOo---

8. Building the physical database from Oracle Designer

8.1 Building a Physical Oracle database - Introduction: At a certain moment in the database design life-cycle, a moment comes when the design team believe that they have captured and defined an accurate physical database model. As we have already emphasised, it is really important to put a lot of effort into the database design process, because it can help avoid a lot of rework later. This is especially true if you are using Oracle Designer as the main tool. Designer takes on a lot of additional data which may be used in application Help messaging, prompts, Error messaging etc. So spend the time with Designer and get the most out of the design cycle.

However, when the moment arrives that the design team believe the physical database design is completed, the next action is the creation of the physical database itself. The physical database will be built in a target Oracle instance and it will be based entirely on the physical database definitions stored in Oracle Designer.

This is an important step in the Design-Development-Build process and needs to be carried out carefully. In a RAD environment, this first "database build" marks an important move towards building the first working prototype.

8.2 RAD Iterations of the database build: In a RAD environment, the first physical database built is considered to be a "prototype", rather than the final version of the database.

Therefore, this first database build is used as the basis of the functional design team's activities in developing the application software. They design and build their user interfaces and batch processes based on the database structures defined in as a result of the Logical and Physical Database Design phases, and generated in this first database build. The functional team may use Oracle Designer to design and build their software prototype, using the physical database built here.

However, Oracle Designer has its limitations when it comes to functional design and software generation. The product basically only allows for the generation of Oracle Forms and Reports and therefore is somewhat limited in terms of software generation. Many alternatives exist: Oracle APEX for example, which cannot currently be generated from Oracle Designer.

8.2.1 Oracle Designer and RAD iterations: As the RAD design process continues, prototypes will be refined by the RAD design group. Indeed, it is certain that this process of refinement will give rise to alterations to the underlying database design as well.

An iteration of the RAD process creates an entirely new database and software build, having a completely new build revision number. If the functional design used to generate software originates in Oracle Designer as Physical Module definitions (Forms and Reports), then generating these iterations are relatively easy to manage. The RAD process flow is as follows:

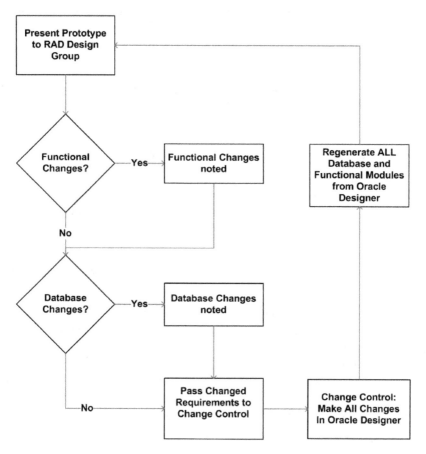

However, if only the database design is stored in Oracle Designer, whilst the software is being produced using some other tool (like Oracle Apex and in native PL/SQL) then a separate functional impact analysis will be necessary for each structural change in the database design.

8.3 Decide on the application schema owner: During design and development, it is an important principle that the target database must be owned by an "application user" or "schema owner". Normally this is an anonymous user with a tightly secured password, created and maintained by the development DBA group.

When a development moves from design to final development and production, the application database owner becomes much more important. The evolution of this user from being just a prototype database owner to becoming a real production database user must be accompanied by a strict tightening of the user Id and associated password.

8.4 Oracle DDL Generators in Oracle Designer: Oracle Designer provides a facility to generate and execute a full set of DDL scripts to create the entire application schema into a target database. This facility is found under the *Generate* menu> *Generate Database from Server Model.*

Here the design team (together with the development DBAs) creates a series of DDL SQL scripts, which are then used to physically create the defined database schema.

These generated scripts can be executed as the application schema owner from within Oracle Designer or in SQL*Plus when connected as the application schema owner.

During execution of these scripts, the development DBAs must take great care that all the defined objects are successfully created. This means that there should be no errors encountered - NONE!

If these scripts are being executed manually in SQL, it is also important to ensure that the generated scripts are executed in the correct order (see below).

Any errors generated during the execution of these build scripts should cause the DBA and designers to investigate and resolve the errors, drop and completely rebuild the schema again. The easiest way to do this is to drop and re-create the application schema owner completely after an iteration of the database build.

8.5 Order of execution: The order of creation of database objects is obviously important. Of course, a table must be created before an index or constraint for that table. There is a logical order to database object creation. This needs to be observed when creating a new database schema, otherwise some objects may fail to be created successfully.

Oracle Designer looks after the order of execution, but if using another tool, it is important that all DDL scripts are executed in the correct order and that all designed objects are successfully created. This is the basic order of Oracle object creation:

- Tablespaces
- Tables
- Constraints
- Indexes
- Views
- Partitions
- Partition Indexes

8.7 Verifying Physical Design versus Physical Build: When using a tool such as Oracle Designer to store and build a physical database design, it is important to ensure that the database has been successfully built. Oracle Designer (and other tools) provides means of comparing the design metadata with the physical database. This comparison is an essential step in the building of the physical database. Before proceeding with any further refinement of the database design, it is essential to ensure that the physical database is identical to the stored design meta-data in Oracle Designer (or any other tool).

8.8 Securing the Physical Database Build: In a RAD environment, the main priority is speed of evolution. The second priority is the ability to "fall back" to the last design iteration, if necessary. This means that it is vitally important to create "frozen" design backups before a new RAD iteration. So, as soon as RAD iterations are completed, it is important to create a complete backup of each RAD revision.

From a database design point of view, this means the following actions:

- Export the physical Database build.
- Export the Oracle Designer repository for the current application.

---oOo---

72

9. Managing Changes during development

One of the most complex issues in software development in a database environment is managing change. Changes come a/ during the design phase, b/ as a result of all types of testing, and c/ as a result of changes in user requirements. All of these types of change can take place during the development and testing, before final user acceptance of a system. The administration of changes during development can form a basis for long-term change management in production.

Changes basically come in 3 forms:

- Changes affecting software only.

- Changes affecting the database only.

- Changes affecting database and software.

We are primarily concerned only with the management of changes in the database. Software change control is a separate subject, with which we will deal in another volume of these guides.

9.1 Strategic issues affecting Change management: There are a number of strategic decisions which affect how well a development team manages change. These are particularly relevant when employing a RAD methodology, where changes are turned around quickly as part of rapid prototyping iterations. The following key roles and tasks need to be considered:

- **Change Controllers:**

    o   Who oversees the entire change process?

    o   How are changes initiated, documented and approved?

    o   How many changes are rolled into a single release?

    o   How are changes controlled chronologically?

- **Custodians:**

    o   Who is the custodian of the physical database design?

    o   Who is the physical owner of the database?

    o   Who controls software and database versioning?

- **Implementers:**
  - How are database changes designed, the designs approved, and changes implemented?
  - Who manages the process of software and database change control during Design and development?
  - How is a database design version controlled? How are versions backed up in case regression is required? Who is responsible?
  - Who controls and makes the changes in the database design?
  - Who controls the final build process after a design change?
  - How is the new database populated with test data?

9.2 Tools for database change control: Changes in design come in all shades: they may be minor, localised, widespread, cosmetic or fundamental. They may affect software and/or database. Changes to a database may or may not affect application software and changes to application software may or may not cause changes to the database. At any rate, all changes require a standardised approach to change control and version management. For this, it is vital to employ a change and version control tool.

Oracle Designer does provide some version management tools, but at this moment in time we cannot recommend the use of Oracle Designer's internal version control utilities. This is because these utilities have little in common and provide no interface with most other software version control systems on the market today. This lack of interface between Designer and other version control systems will rapidly become an obstacle. A better strategy is to use a generic version control system that also works for the entire design and development team - including the software developers.

Therefore, we strongly suggest using one of the common 3rd party tools such as VSS, Subversion, Clearcase, or CVS (etc.) to store the generated DDL scripts for each database version that emerges from a change in Oracle Designer. This means that after every set of RAD authorised changes, a complete set of DDL creation scripts is generated from Designer, and named to reflect its current version and date. These files are then checked into your chosen version control system with the appropriate new version number allocated. We would also suggest exporting and storing a full copy of each previous version of the database in such a tool, in case an urgent version regression is required.

9.3 How are changes managed in RAD? In a RAD environment, speed of change is everything. Traditional change control procedures won't work using a RAD methodology, because the time between request and rebuild is too great. The power of RAD lies in being able to deliver software and database revision with very little delay between request and delivery. This priority affects the process of managing change during development as follows:

- A single revision should not include too many changes. Ideally RAD cycles should not exceed 7 days. Therefore, it is better to have many short RAD cycles rather than a few very long cycles. The RAD participants will become disengaged from the design process if the cycles take too long. The RAD Project Manager therefore has to ensure that revisions are not so large that they cannot be completed in a reasonable time (one week, for example). If necessary, changes should be postponed to the next RAD revision meeting. Gradually revisions will become smaller in number and impact.

- Each change should be clearly defined in writing during the RAD review, and it should also be technically evaluated by the designers on the spot. The basic design change should be determined during the RAD review and documented immediately. This represents the change being passed to change control.

- All changes coming from a RAD review are passed to the Change Controller for impact analysis, commentary, and initiation. After analysis, changes are signed off for action and the Change Controller manages the changes through the entire change process, from design to implementation.

9.4 Who does what during a change? Returning to the above questions about roles in the change process, here are some general rules about responsibilities:

- Change carries high risks, is complicated and must be carefully controlled

- Everyone must be clear about their role and responsibility in the change process and stick to their part.

The following explains the key responsibilities:

9.4.1 Change Controller:

- **Who oversees the entire change process?** One person should be nominated to be the role of "Change Controller". In a RAD environment, this person will be close to the Development Team leader.

- **How are changes initiated, documented and approved?** Changes are the outcome of RAD reviews and are produced under the control of the RAD team leaders. They are defined and documented during the RAD reviews. Potential technical solutions are also documented during these reviews. The changes are approved for investigation and impact analysis during the RAD review.

- **-How many changes are rolled into a single release?** The number of changes rolled up into a single release depends on the size of the design and development team and the time in between RAD reviews. A typical RAD iteration shouldn't exceed a week (in general). Based on the chosen length of the release cycle, the RAD team leader must limit the number of changes to what is practically possible for the team to evaluate, design, build and implement in the time between reviews.

- **How are database changes controlled chronologically?** There is a possibility that changes made as a result of one RAD request, are impacted by a later request. It is important in a RAD environment to fully implement changes in a strictly chronological order.

- **How are conflicting design changes managed?** Obvious contradictions or conflicts between changes should be rejected from the current change iteration and referred back to the RAD design team for clarification in the next RAD review.

9.4.2 Custodians of the database and its versions:

- **Who is the custodian of the physical database design?** The physical design of the database (stored in Oracle Designer or another tool) is the responsibility of the senior Development DBA. This responsibility includes guaranteeing that the Oracle Designer (or other) repository is backed up on a regular basis and that version control of changed versions of the database is properly implemented and secure.

- **Who is the physical owner of the physical database?** The physical database is the responsibility of the senior Development DBA. After every release of the database, the senior DBA must ensure that a backup is made of the old and new database builds and designs. These must be defined and stored, using the project version control system in the following way:

- o complete set of DDL scripts for the database build

- o Oracle export file of the last version of the database as an export file (with data if required).

- o Oracle export file of the new version of the database as an export file.

- o Complete export file of the new and old Oracle Designer (or other design repository) database definitions.

- **Who manages the process of software and database change control during Design and development?** Ultimately, the responsibility for managing the RAD process belongs to the Development Team Leader, but in fact the change process is driven and controlled by the Change Controller who reports to the Development Team Leader. The Change Controller takes over the management of all changes emerging from the RAD reviews. This is a vital role which involves impact analysis of each change, liaising with designers and developers and ensuring that changes are implemented in a logical order, and that illogical requests are recycled to the RAD Design Team for re-evaluation.

- **Who controls software and database versioning during Design and development?** Before and after software and database changes are made, it is important to manage the configuration control of the current version of the database (and application software). This is the role of the Release and Version Controller. This person effectively manages the version control system and ensures that every new build is correctly registered and managed by the chosen version control system. This involves liaising with the Development DBA to ensure that the system contains the full set of versioned files (DDL scripts, database and design exports (see above)).

9.4.3 Implementers:

- **How are database changes evaluated, designed, approved, and implemented?** During a RAD review, user representatives evaluate the latest system prototype and make suggestions and requests to the Design and Development for changes. These are typically evaluated "on the spot", with the help of the business analyst, the

77

database designer and the software designer in the RAD team. Together, the user's requirement is evaluated to see if it is valid and if it fits within the terms of the System Requirements definition. If the requirement is valid, the user, analyst and designers work together to further define the user requirement and suggestions for potential solutions. This is documented during the RAD review and signed off by User and Development managers at the conclusion of the RAD review.

When a RAD review is completed all of the agreed changes pass to the Change Controller. The role of the Change Controller is as follows:

- o Liaise with Development DBAs and Software Team Leader.

- o Carry out an impact analysis of each change together with DBA and Software Team lead.

- o Define and document database and software design changes for each change.

- o Define a new application revision (database and software) and define which changes are to be included in the revision.

- o Ensure that the changes are passed to the Design and Development teams.

- o Monitor and progress chase changes in design.

- o Review design changes and approve the changes.

- o Prepare for the implementation of a new revision (audit backups etc).

- o Oversee the physical implementation of a new revision.

- o Communicate the availability of the new revision to users / testers etc.

- o Ensure that the new revision is correctly version controlled (via the Release Controller).

- **Who is responsible for database version control?** Every development project employs at least one person who is responsible for the critical task of managing change, implementing new versions and securing copies of old versions. In our suggested RAD hierarchy this role would be occupied by the "Release and

Version Controller", working directly for the project "Change Controller", although these may be the same person in reality.

- **How is a database design version controlled?** After changes have been identified and implemented in the database design, they are then generated into a series of DDL files, an export of the latest (frozen) design repository and an export of the newly generated database scheme. The Release and Version controller is responsible for collecting these files and checking them into the chosen project configuration control system.

In terms of version numbering, there are lots of quite convoluted version models in use. However, in general, simplicity is best with version control. A suggestion for an easy to understand version control system might be something of the format:

Vn.mmm

Where: V refers to version, n=0 during development and n=1 after production, mmm= RAD change iteration in development and major release in production.

Thus a system versioned V0.023 would indicate development system, after RAD review 23. A system versioned V1.002 would indicate production system, after change package 2.

Whatever version number system you use, all the DDL and export files collected by the Release and Version Controller should be named to reflect their current revision number, and these revision numbers should also be used in the configuration control system.

- **How are database versions backed up in case regression is required?**

After every new release the following files are collected and stored in the configuration control system and in a separate safe destination:

- o   complete set of DDL scripts for the database build.

- o   Oracle export files of the last version of the database as an export file (with data if required).

- o   Oracle export file of the new version of the database as an export file.

- o   complete export file of the new and old Oracle Designer (or other design repository) database definitions.

- **Who controls and makes the changes in the database design?** The final responsibility for implementing a change in the development database design is the Development DBA. This person must be convinced that the changes are logical and that their impact has been fully evaluated. The Development DBA gives the final approval to the physical schema model. In production, a similar regime exists: no changes may take place to a production data model or database without the explicit consent and involvement of the schema owner, who is normally a member of the system DBA group.

- **Who controls the final build process after a design change**? The technical implications of building a new database after a design change mean that this task is also the domain of the Development DBA. The DBA may decide to carry out a complete database rebuild (unlikely), or just create the necessary scripts to alter the database to implement a set of limited changes (more likely). However, because data may need to be preserved, the scenario for even simple changes can rapidly become complicated. Thus, this role needs to reside with the DBA.

- **How is the new database populated with test data?** And on the subject of preserving data after a database change, this can often present a challenge when there are fundamental changes in data structure.

  Very often a RAD team are using fixed datasets to test iterations of the RAD design and build. If major changes are made to the underlying database structure during development, there is a risk that test data may be lost. The development DBA is responsible for building the test data sets being used and ensuring that new database builds have a full set of data available to both development and user teams.

  To do this the DBA will generally create a mirror of the tables being altered as a result of a RAD review. These mirror tables will contain the old data but stored in a separate schema (owned by a separate user). When the changes are implemented, the DBA will then construct the necessary scripts to transfer data from the mirrored tables to the newly altered tables.

---o0o---

10. Glossary of Terms

APEX: Apex is Oracle Application Express, an Oracle product that has been a long time in development and is the latest in a set of Oracle front-end design and development tools. APEX is embedded and integrated into the application database and provides a sophisticated toolkit for rapid web application development against an Oracle database. APEX is basically a web front end development environment, based on an Oracle database. For an experienced developer it can be a very good tool to produce a resilient dynamic html web-based front-end. Despite the claims of Oracle, it is really *not* a development tool for a novice. However, it is an excellent product and has rapidly replaced Oracle Forms and Reports as the front-end of choice for many Oracle applications where a web interface is needed.

Constraints (database constraints): Constraints are rules of *data integrity* for a database that limit the acceptable data values for a table. They are the optional schema objects that depend on a table. The existence of a table without any constraint is possible, but the existence of a constraint without any table is not possible.

Constraints enforce business rules in a database. If a constraint is violated during a transaction, the transaction will fail, be rolled-back and a specific error occurs.

Constraints can be created along with the table in the CREATE TABLE statement. Addition and deletion of constraints can be done in the ALTER TABLE statement. The following types of constraints are available in Oracle Database:

- **NOT NULL:** It enforces that a column, declared as not null, cannot have any NULL values. For example, if an employee's hire date is not known, then that employee may not be considered as a valid employee.

- **UNIQUE:** It ensures that columns protected by this constraint cannot have duplicate values.

- **PRIMARY KEY:** It is responsible for uniquely identifying a row in a table. A table can have only one PRIMARY KEY constraint. A PRIMARY KEY constraint wholly includes both the NOT NULL and UNIQUE constraints. It is enforced with an index on all columns in the key.

- **FOREIGN KEY:** It is also known as referential integrity constraint. It enforces that values referenced in one table, are defined in another table. It establishes a parent-child or reference-dependent relationship between the two tables.

- **CHECK:** It enforces that columns must meet a specific condition that is evaluated to a Boolean value. If the value evaluates to false, then the database will raise an exception and not allow the INSERT and UPDATE statements to operate on columns.

DBA: A Database Administrator: This is the person (database "role") responsible for the installation, configuration, upgrade, administration, monitoring and maintenance of (Oracle) databases within an organisation or in a development project. The role includes the design and development of database strategies, database monitoring, database performance tuning and capacity planning for future expansion. A DBA is also responsible for the planning, co-ordination and implementation of security measures to safeguard controlled access to the database, database availability and database backup and failure management.

Edgar Codd (1923 - 2003) was an English computer scientist who, while working for IBM, invented the relational model for database management, the theoretical basis for relational databases. The relational model, a very influential general theory of data management, remains his most important achievement.

Denormalization: This is the process of grouping data from several related tables into a single "denormalized" table. In some cases, denormalization is a means of addressing query performance. OLAP type applications often denormalize data to achieve complex queries with reasonable response times. A normalized design will store different, but related, pieces of information in separate logical tables which are, therefore, related. Completing a database query that draws information from several tables (using a join operation) can be slow. If many relations are joined, it may be unusable in an OLAP application and denormalization may be the only solution.

DDL: Data Definition Language: Data definition language syntax is used to define data structures, especially database schemas. Examples of DDL include object creation statements such as:

"CREATE TABLE INVOICE_HEADERS......."

DML: Data Manipulation Language: This is a family of syntax elements in SQL which are used for inserting, updating and deleting data in a database. Read-only queries of data, (select, in SQL) are also considered a component of DML. Examples of DML include select statements such as:

```
SELECT * FROM INVOICE_LINES
WHERE INVOICE_NO = '7627682'...
```

Function index: Prior to Oracle 8i, if a SQL query used any kind of function on a column in the WHERE clause, then the SQL Optimizer would use a full scan of the table and making a comparison between the clause and the function calculated column value.

For example, in the following SQL statement, the index on INVOICE_NO would be ignored by the SQL Optimizer, because the statement is making a comparison with the left substring (function derivative) of the table's column and *not* the natural column value which is actually stored in the index. The index is therefore useless and a full table scan ensues:

```
SELECT * FROM INVOICE_LINES
WHERE left(INVOICE_NO,1,7) = '7627682'...
```

Oracle 8i solved this problem by allowing a designer to create a "Function Index" for commonly used function queries like the example. In the same example we would create a function index on INVOICE_NO in the INVOICES table based on the left substring as follows:

```
CREATE INDEX INVOICE_LEFT_7 ON
INVOICES(left(INVOICE_NO,1,7));
```

When the same query is executed, the Optimizer chooses to search the new index we created (INVOICE_LEFT_7) and proceeds to avoid a lengthy full table scan.

Index: An Index is an Oracle database object associated with a table. Indexes provide improved access to table rows by storing sorted values from specific columns and using those sorted values to find associated table rows more easily.

This means that data can be found without having to look at more than a fraction of the total rows within a table. Indexes are optional, but generally associated with primary and unique keys and often with foreign key columns. The use of indexes is not always positive. An index may improve data retrieval speed, but inserting data is less efficient, because every new record means that one or more indexes need to be updated. This reduces performance, which can be a disadvantage for OLTP database processing. However, in a data warehouse environment (where transaction processing doesn't happen), indexes can be used without too much consideration and generally yield performance improvements.

Instance (Oracle instance): A database instance is a set of memory structures that manage database files. A database is a set of physical files on disk, created by the "CREATE DATABASE" statement. The instance manages its associated data and serves the users of the database. Every running Oracle database is associated with at least one Oracle database instance.

Methodologies - project methodologies, software engineering techniques: A software development methodology is a framework used to structure, plan, and control the process of development of an information system. A methodology includes the definition of software deliverables that a project team will develop as part of a software application. There are many methodologies, for example: Prototyping, Rapid Application Development, Waterfall methodology, Spiral Methodology, Incremental Methodology etc. In an Oracle environment, a RAD or Prototyping approach works best, in general. See RAD below.

Non-unique index: You can use Non-unique indexes to improve the performance of data access, when the values of the columns in the index are not necessarily unique.

Advice: Do not create Non-unique indexes on very small tables because scans of small tables alone are usually more efficient than using an index and then also accessing the table.

Normalization: One of the underlying mathematical principles in Codd's relational theory is that of normalization of data. In relational database design, normalization is a process which takes place during and after the process of Entity-Relationship modelling, where a logical data model is being transformed into a physical data model, before being turned into a physical database.

Despite being so fundamental to relational design, data normalization is still widely misunderstood by Users, Analysts, Designers and Developers.

The primary objectives of data normalization are the removal of redundancy and dependency. This means that when data is inserted, updated or deleted, these processes only take place once in each table. Normalization works by dividing large entities or tables into smaller (less redundant) entities (tables) and by amalgamating entities which have a shared one-to one relationship.

There are three concepts of data normalization referred to as "first, second and third normal form". Generally speaking, the objective of a relational database designer is to define a database which conforms to "Third Normal Form". However, there are many exceptions to this objective which we will explore in a later volume, when discussing database performance.

For now, here are the rules for each level of data normalization:

- **First Normal Form** states that a "Table faithfully represents a relation, primarily meaning it has at least one candidate key".

- So, first normal form deals really with the "shape" of a record type. Under first normal form, all occurrences of a record type must contain the same number of fields. First normal form excludes repeating fields and groups. This basically means that repeating data must be removed from a table to eliminate repeating groups of data. Thus, if we had an Invoice table which incorporated invoice line and invoice header data in the same records, we would need to separate the data into two tables, in order to make it conform to first normal form.

- **Second Normal Form** states that "no non-prime attribute in the table is functionally dependent on a proper subset of any candidate key".

  So, the objective here to bring data to 2nd Normal form is to remove part key dependents, the data that is *partly* dependent on a key. For example, in our invoice lines table, we would not include the attributes "Product price" or "Product description", because these attributes ought to be part of a separate "Products" table if our database were normalised to 2nd Normal form.

- **Third Normal Form** states that every non-prime attribute is non-transitively dependent on every candidate key in the table. The attributes that do not contribute to the description of the primary key are removed from the table. In other words, no transitive dependency is allowed.

  The objective here is to remove non-key dependencies, i.e. data that is not dependent on other keys. So, are any of the attributes primarily dependent on one of the other non-key attributes rather than the design key? In our Invoice Header example, Customer

Name, Address and Tax Id would be separated into a separate Customer table. Only the Customer number would appear in the Invoice Header table, and so on.

Object-Relational database: An object-relational database (ORD), or object-relational database management system (ORDBMS), is a database management system (DBMS) similar to a relational database, but with an object-oriented database model: objects, classes and inheritance are directly supported in database schemas and in the query language. In addition, just as with proper relational systems, it supports extension of the data model with custom data-types and methods. Oracle can be used as an Object-Relational database.

An Object-Relational database can be said to provide a middle ground between relational databases and object-oriented databases (OODBMS). In object-relational databases, the approach is essentially that of relational databases: the data resides in the database and is manipulated collectively with queries in a query language; at the other extreme are OODBMS's in which the database is essentially a persistent object store for software written in an object-oriented programming language, with a programming API for storing and retrieving objects, and little or no specific support for querying.

OLAP: On-line Analytical Processing: This is a type or part of a system, characterized by a relatively low volume of transactions. Queries are often very complex and involve aggregations. For OLAP systems a response time is a measure of effectiveness. OLAP applications are widely used by Data Mining techniques. In an OLAP database there is aggregated, historical data, stored in multi-dimensional schemas (usually star schema) which may be heavily denormalized.

OLTP: On-line Transaction processing: This is a type or part of a system which is characterized by a large number of short on-line transactions (INSERT, UPDATE, and DELETE). The main emphasis for OLTP systems is put on very fast query processing, maintaining data integrity in multi-access environments and an effectiveness measured by the number of transactions per second. OLTP is the "system opposite" of OLAP (On-line Analytical Processing), which is used to aggregate and obtain information rather than make user transactions.

PL/SQL: Procedural Language/Structured Query Language (PL/SQL) is Oracle's procedural extension language for SQL and the Oracle database. SQL is limited by not having any procedure syntax.

The concept of "if" simply doesn't exist in SQL. SQL is a set language and deals only with the basic transactional events of INSERT, UPDATE, and DELETE, and of course, the basic query syntax of SELECT.

Prior to PL/SQL, programmers were obliged to "wrap up" tracts of SQL in other 3G languages (which Oracle provided) such as Pro*C, Pro*Cobol, etc. Whilst this worked fine, Oracle needed a new procedural language which could be stored and executed from within the database itself and PL/SQL was therefore released with Oracle version 7. It has a full set of procedural syntax and is a relatively easy language to use. Needless to say the PL/SQL is very much biased towards database processing and has a limited amount of other non-dataset I/O facilities.

Procedures and Triggers: PL/SQL program units can be stored as procedures and triggers in the database. This is a very useful way of controlling the behaviour of a table during a DML transaction. For example, imagine that an Order Header table also stores the total value for all its Order Lines as a denormalized column. When a new order line is added, this total most be recalculated and the Order Header table updated. The same is true when an Order line is deleted or updated. Again, the order header total value needs to be recalculated and the Order Header table kept up-to-date with the new total value.

- This scenario is ideally managed using 3 triggers on the Order Line table which will "fire" ON-INSERT, ON-UPDATE, and ON-DELETE.

- Each of these triggers then calls a stored PL/SQL procedure, called, for example, RECALCULATE_ORDER_TOTAL.

- This procedure will recalculate the sum of the ORDER_LINE_VALUE and then issue an UPDATE of the ORDER_HEADER table to update the stored total value.

Performance: Oracle performance is usually measured by processing cycle times, or data throughput rates. Oracle performance can be a critical issue in very large databases (VLDB), where mission critical tasks can be delayed by poor processing times. Also, performance is not a static issue. Performance may degrade over time as data volumes or the number of user processes increase, or as tables or indexes become more and more disorganised. Performance is generally affected by the following issues: Appropriate server sizing, careful Oracle instance configuration, optimal physical database design (indexes, partitioning etc), SQL software design (optimal access path for retrieving data), and the quality and frequency of database maintenance.

Primary and unique keys - the differences: In logical database design, a normalised entity is allocated a Unique Identifier (UID). This UID consists of one or more attributes which, taken together, can be used to uniquely identify one instance of that entity (or one record in a table).

For example, in a Human Resources database this unique identifier might be Social Security Number or some artificial "surrogate" key created by the company, such as Employee Id. Very often, an entity has more than one possible unique identifier. Name, date of birth and place of birth can perhaps be used as a unique id in some applications. During the transition from logical design to physical design, certain decisions need to be made about these identifiers. One of them must be selected as the Primary Key of the table, and the remaining alternative unique identifiers must be defined as unique keys. A primary key is the main method by which a record is identified. Unique keys are alternate methods of identifying a record. Both types of key MUST be unique, and the database will enforce this uniqueness using Primary and Unique Key Constraints, which basically enforce the uniqueness using Unique Indexes on the defined columns. It is therefore imperative to be absolutely sure about the definition of these keys during the Oracle database design phase.

Rapid Application Development (RAD): Rapid application development is a term originally used to describe a software development process introduced by James Martin, the Systems Design researcher, in 1991. RAD is a software development methodology, which involves iterative design and development and the construction of prototypes. The basic principles of RAD are:

- Key objective is for fast development and delivery of a high quality system with a relatively low investment.

- RAD aims to produce high quality systems quickly, primarily via iterative Prototyping, active user involvement, and computerized development tools. These tools may include GUI builders, Computer Aided Software Engineering (CASE) tools (in Oracle this would be Oracle Designer or a similar tool), Database Management Systems (DBMS), fourth-generation programming languages (in Oracle this may be PL/SQL), code generators (in Oracle this could be APEX, Oracle Forms, Reports, JDeveloper etc.) , and object-oriented techniques (in Oracle this would be the object-relational ability to embed code and validation properties in the database, associated with particular tables).

- Active user involvement is imperative. It generally includes a concept of joint application design (JAD), where users are intensely involved in system design, via structured workshops.

- Standard systems analysis and design methods can be fitted into a RAD framework.

- In RAD, the key emphasis is on fulfilling the business need, while technological or engineering excellence is of lesser importance.

- Project control involves prioritizing development and defining delivery deadlines or "timeboxes". If the project starts to slip, emphasis is on reducing requirements to fit the timebox, not in increasing the deadline. In a slipping schedule, non-essentials are abandoned.

- RAD attempts to reduce inherent project risk by breaking a project into smaller segments and providing more ease-of-change during the development process.

- RAD iteratively produces production software, as opposed to throwaway prototypes. Each RAD recursion is a working system. Each recursion seeks to come closer to the consensus of user requirements.

- RAD produces the documentation necessary to facilitate future development and maintenance.

Relationship matrix: A relationship matrix is a graphical representation, which allows an analyst to establish an initial matrix of all possible relationships between the entities in a data model. The matrix makes a comparison between all entities and all other entities in the model. When a relationship is found to exist between Table A and Table X then the intersection of these two tables is marked to indicate the presence of a relationship. The following example indicates how this matrix is constructed:

	Buyer	Requester	Approver	Purchase Requisition	Purchase Req. Item
Buyer		X		X	
Requester	X			X	
Approver				X	
Purchase Requisition	X	X	X		X
Purchase Req. Item				X	

An Entity-Relationship Matrix only reflects that a
relationship of some kind may exist.

Rollback: Use the ROLLBACK statement to undo work done in the current transaction, or to manually undo the work done by an in-doubt distributed transaction. If a transaction or set of transactions has been done on a set of table data, it can be reverted in the same session using the ROLLBACK command. Rollback is the transactional opposite to COMMIT.

Schema: A schema is the set of objects (tables, views, indexes, etc) that belong to a user account. The word is also often used as another way to refer to an Oracle user.

Schema diagram: In database design a schema diagram is a schematic, similar to an E-R diagram. The difference is that a schema diagram shows physical database objects such as tables, views, primary and foreign keys etc., rather than logical entities and relationships.

A schema diagram is normally produced after an E-R model has been fully normalised, but before the physical database has been built. The schema diagram is a very useful tool for developers. It operates like a database "map", because it allows them to see exactly where and how data may be extracted and maintained in the physical database.

A schema diagram is produced using a tool such as Oracle Designer, (Toad and other tools also produce Schema diagrams, but none are as well integrated into the Oracle database as the Designer product).

Security data and functional: Oracle provides very granular and very safe built-in security functions, which operate at a role, user, privilege, object, row, and column level.

- **Basic User Functional Privileges:** When a user account is created, they are allocated certain group privileges. A normal operational user would be allocated so-called CONNECT privileges. This would not allow them to create private database objects such as tables, but would allow them to connect to the database as a basic user. A developer would be granted RESOURCE privilege which allows them to use DML commands, and a DBA would receive DBA privilege which gives them the right to create database objects and grant privileges on them to others, etc.

- **Roles and Tables:** When tables have been created as part of a database build, they are only accessible to the application owner user and the DBA. No-one else has any form of access to these tables. They must first be granted explicit access to these tables to perform the explicit operations SELECT, INSERT, UPDATE, DELETE.

  So, in addition to granting users these basic roles, a database administrator and the application designer would also define and create a matrix of user roles into which all physical users would fall. For example, a role of "Invoice Entry" would

  "GRANT SELECT, INSERT, UPDATE, DELETE on INVOICE_HEADERS to INVOICE_ENTRY_ROLE"

  "GRANT SELECT, INSERT, UPDATE, DELETE on INVOICE_LINES to INVOICE_ENTRY_ROLE"

- **Roles and Users:** Any new user joining the Invoice entry team would then be granted this role and thus inherit its privileges as follows:

  "GRANT INVOICE_ENTRY_ROLE to NEW_USER"

The effect of this would be that this user would have the right to insert, update, delete and select from the INVOICE_HEADERS and INVOICE_LINES tables.

- **Restricting Data access:** A user or role can be explicitly excluded from any or all forms of access to a particular dataset within a table, using various methods, including database views or the use of Virtual Private Database (VPD). This enables you to create security policies to control database access at the row and column level. Essentially, Oracle Virtual Private Database adds a dynamic WHERE clause to a SQL statement that is issued against the table, view, or synonym to which an Oracle Virtual Private Database security policy was applied.

From these simple examples we can see that Oracle provides an extremely safe and very granular level of security. The whole subject of security is an important component in application design, and the priority is to design a simple but resilient method of administrating users, which guarantees data and functional security.

SQL*Plus (SQL pronounced "Sequel"): SQL*Plus is the most basic Oracle Database utility, with a basic command-line interface. It is an Oracle product based on the ANSI standard SQL (Structured Query Language). The primary command syntax is divided into two parts:

- **DDL:** Data definition language, used to create and modify database objects, e.g. "CREATE TABLE INVOICES..."

- **DML:** Data modification language, used to INSERT, UPDATE, DELETE and SELECT from existing database objects, such as tables and views etc., e.g.

    "SELECT * FROM INVOICES WHERE INVOICE_NO = '123456'..."

Unique Index: Unique indexes are used to ensure that no identical key values are stored in a table. When we create a table that contains a primary key, we must also create a unique index for that table on the primary key. Unique indexes are also created on other unique keys defined for a table.

User Requirements documentation (URD): is a document used in software engineering that specifies the requirements the user expects from software to be constructed in a software project.

An important and difficult step of designing a software product is determining what the customer actually wants it to do. This is because often a customer is not able to communicate the entirety of their requirements, and the information they provide may be incomplete, inaccurate and conflicting. The responsibility of completely understanding what the customer wants falls to the providers of the product.

For a software project's success, it is critical that the user requirements be documented as specifically and unambiguously as possible. Once the required information is completely gathered, it is documented in a URD. This should define the exact functionality of the proposed software system. This document often becomes part of the contractual agreement between a customer and a software provider and is therefore an important link between the legal and design requirements of a system. Thus, a customer cannot demand features not in the URD and a developer cannot claim the product is ready if it does not satisfy some part of the URD. The URD can be used as a guide to planning costs, timetables, milestones, testing, and implementation. The explicit nature of the URD allows customers to show it to various stakeholders to make sure all necessary features are described.

Formulating a URD requires negotiation to determine what is technically and economically feasible. Preparing a URD requires both software technical skills and interpersonal and communication skills.

Often a URD includes priority ranking for each requirement. A typical system might be as follows:

- M Mandatory requirement. This feature must be built into the final system.

- D Desirable requirement. This feature should be built into the final system, unless the cost is too high.

- O Optional requirement.

- E Possible future enhancement.

Validation of data: Data validation is the process by which data, which is incoming to a system, is tested to ensure that it conforms to the basic business rules of the system. These business rules include low level testing of the data type (alpha or numeric), the form of the data (length etc). The validation may also include testing that data is related to an existing parent record, that the keys of a record are unique, and that columns within a record conform with various cross-validation rules, specific to the business. In Oracle, much of the data validation process is embedded in the database itself, within database primary, unique and foreign key constraints and does not need to be separately coded.

---o0o---

About the author

Malcolm Coxall, the author, is a business and IT systems analyst and consultant with more than 30 years freelance experience in Europe and the Middle East. Malcolm has worked in Oracle systems design and development for the last 25 years as a developer, business analyst, database designer, DBA, systems administrator, team lead and project manager.

With experience working for many of the world's largest corporate and institutional players, as well as for several government and international agencies, Malcolm has extensive hands-on experience in designing and building large-scale Oracle systems in many diverse vertical markets such as banking, oil, defence, telecoms, manufacturing, mining, food, agriculture, aerospace, and engineering.

Malcolm also writes and publishes books, papers and articles on human system design, sociology, environmental economics, sustainable technology and technology in environmental protection and food production.

Malcolm lives in southern Spain from where he continues his freelance Oracle consultancy and his writing, whilst managing the family's organic farm.

---oOo---

www.ingramcontent.com/pod-product-compliance
Lightning Source LLC
LaVergne TN
LVHW052308060326
832902LV00021B/3770